PLAYGROUND DESIGN

PLAYGROUND DESIGN

Outdoor Environments for Learning and Development

Aase Eriksen, M.Arch., Ph.D.

VNR Van Nostrand Reinhold Company
New York

Copyright © 1985 by Van Nostrand Reinhold Company Inc.
Library of Congress Catalog Card Number 85-6037
ISBN 0-442-22257-2

Printed in the United States of America

Designed by Loudan Enterprises

Van Nostrand Reinhold Company Inc.
135 West 50th Street
New York, New York 10020

Van Nostrand Reinhold Company Limited
Molly Millars Lane
Wokingham, Berkshire RG11 2PY, England

Van Nostrand Reinhold
480 La Trobe Street
Melbourne, Victoria 3000, Australia

Macmillan of Canada
Division of Canada Publishing Corporation
164 Commander Boulevard
Agincourt, Ontario M1S 3C7, Canada

16 15 14 13 12 11 10 9 8 7 6 5 4 3 2 1

Library of Congress Cataloging in Publication Data

Eriksen, Aase.
  Playground design.

  Bibliography: p.
  Includes index.
  1. Playgrounds—Design and construction.
  2. Playgrounds—United States—Design and construction.
  3. Playgrounds—Michigan—Grand Rapids—Design and
construction—Case studies. I. Title.
GV425.E74 1985   711'.558   85-6037
ISBN 0-442-22257-2

Contents

Acknowledgments

This book is written in gratitude to all the thousands of collaborators—
the children with whom I have worked over the years.

I also want to thank:

- K. Helveg-Petersen, former Minister of Culture and of Education
  Denmark, and Sir Peter Shepheard, Architect, Landscape Architect
  of London and Philadelphia, who over the years supported my work
  in architecture and education. Their vision of life, and concern for
  children and the young, have been an inspiration.
- Frederik Bredahl-Petersen, Anthropologist, whose vision of man and
  culture helped me in my cross-cultural work with children and
  adults.
- Milton J. Miller, Associate Superintendent of Schools in Grand
  Rapids, Michigan, who dared to take on a true *People Designing
  Places* project.
- Lilly Helveg-Petersen, teacher and former Mayor of Copenhagen,
  who supported and encouraged me in my work with built-
  environment awareness education.
- John Carstens, Ph.D., without whose help in researching and edit-
  ing, this book would not have been completed.
- Patricia Coyne, for her organization and typing of this book, and for
  her loyal help and support through the years.

I hope this book will help to give children what they need and want—
Playscapes.

Introduction

Although playground design has received serious attention from concerned parents, educators, and architects in the past thirty years, even a casual look at most of our nation's playgrounds should convince the observer of the great need for new and better-designed playgrounds for our children.

By far the majority of America's playgrounds are hard-surfaced areas with open spaces for ball games and, scattered here and there, random groupings of standard play equipment such as swings, seesaws, and monkey bars. If the playground is on a school site, it is usually surrounded by a high chain-link fence, which protects it against after-school use but also makes it resemble a prison yard. Such unattractive playgrounds seem to invite vandalism, and it is not uncommon to see swing chains dangling without seats and seesaws painted with graffiti. Even worse, such playgrounds are dangerous. Unsafe equipment and the hard surfaces so often used beneath it have been shown to contribute to serious, even fatal, accidents and falls.

The sad condition of many of our traditional playgrounds and the fact that such playgrounds often stand empty and neglected by the children have led some critics to speak out against *all* playgrounds. They argue that children can and will play at any time, in any setting, even in the most littered vacant lot in a city. Therefore, playgrounds as spaces specifically set aside for children are unnecessary, even undesirable, as they limit children's creativity. After all, children played whenever and wherever they could centuries before the first playground was created without the benefit of fancy play equipment (that is, we should remember, *if* they were allowed to play at all, given their full-time work of helping with the family's livelihood).

While it may be true that children do play anywhere, it does not therefore follow that playgrounds are unnecessary, even though the traditional playground is admittedly a waste of space when locked against children's use, especially if it remains as dangerous as so many are. Rather, for many reasons, children *do* need carefully designed spaces set aside for their play activities.

Young children in particular benefit from the shelter and protection provided by a separate, enticing, varied play space. In fact, rather than stifling their creativity, a properly designed play environment stimulates children's learning and development. Certainly a playground that provides safe equipment for physical and fantasy play, as well as landscaped areas for nature play, is preferable to the vacant lot full of rusty cans or the street where ball games must be interrupted by passing traffic.

This book proposes the development of landscaped environments for play that combine a variety of settings for many different play activities.

Such a play environment provides an important means to stimulate the growth of the "whole child," that is, the development of the child's physical, emotional, social, and intellectual abilities. In addition, such a play environment becomes an amenity to the community, creating a green and inviting space for adults and children alike.

The designs for such play environments should be adaptable to the two settings most commonly used for playgrounds in America. First are those playgrounds that are connected with institutions, such as schools or day-care centers, where supervision and guidance during play activities can be provided by teachers or interested adults. These playgrounds may also be used without supervision if they remain open after school, as they should be. The other playground setting is the public park, which is likewise generally used without supervision. A playground design that could be used in both circumstances would combine ease of supervision and safety of play with a variety of activity settings that appeal to children of different ages.

Both the community park and the playscape—described in chapters 5 and 6 of this book—show the rich and varied possibilities that exist for redesigning school sites and traditional playgrounds into appealing recreational and play environments. However, to understand these concepts fully, it is first important to look at the considerations taken into account before these designs were created.

Chapter 1 thus begins with a description of the learning and development of children that any well-designed play environment should support and stimulate. The material upon which this chapter is based covers the last 150 years of research into childhood growth, learning, and development.

Chapters 2 through 4 relate the history of playgrounds and examine both the positive aspects and the shortcomings of the many playground designs that have been used in the past. These chapters look at the history of the traditional playground, the development of the adventure playground concept, and the new directions that playground design has taken in the past thirty years.

Chapter 5 then turns to the creation of community parks and recreation areas on school sites as a means of providing both ideal play environments for children and recreational opportunities for neighborhood adults. Of special importance is the design process suggested for creating such sites. It calls for the active involvement of community residents and interest groups, including children, in the design of the community park.

Chapter 6 draws on the material in the previous chapters to illustrate the concepts of the *playscape*—the outdoor play environment that supports children's development through the provision of many and varied activity settings and appropriate play equipment.

The case studies that are reported in chapters 5 and 6 are taken from a Grand Rapids, Michigan, project. In this imaginative undertaking, the community park called Central Park and the Fountain Elementary School Playscape for preschool and elementary school children are built on a school site, using the participatory design process. Each provides a green, landscaped space in the middle of an urban environment.

Chapter 1.

Learning and Development through Play

A large body of literature—both theoretical and experiential—exists on childhood learning and development and provides an important base for understanding the influence of the environment on the life of a child. The design of any physical environment for children—including a setting for play—should take this large body of knowledge into account. The material for this chapter was drawn from extensive research into the writings of the major thinkers and researchers on childhood learning and development over the past 150 years. The material is summarized here to provide a general background for the designer of any play environment for children ranging from early childhood to approximately twelve years of age.

Theorists and researchers who have analyzed childhood development, such as Friedrich Froebel, John Dewey, Rudolf Steiner, Maria Montessori, Jean Piaget, and Susan Isaacs, agree on several principles of child development, including the importance of play. No environment for children—including a play space—should be designed without these principles in mind.

These theorists and researchers agree that healthy growth and development—including physical, emotional, social, and intellectual growth—is based on stimulating learning experiences that arouse the learner's interest. These principles are based on a belief in the natural curiosity of children and their innate desire and ability to learn.

Play is certainly an area of activity in which children's natural curiosity usually guides what they will learn. They will want to know many things—what is it? why? how? can I do it?—as they explore a nature area, walk through a maze, or experiment with a rope ladder. Play should be controlled by the children's own interests. They pursue whatever arouses their curiosity as they are attracted by this object or diverted by that object.

The theorists and researchers also generally agree that learning and development should be personally relevant, arising from and relating to the child's own experience. Children should proceed at their own individual pace and thus develop a sense of independence and self-worth. If children are ready for a particular stage of physical or social development, they will likely choose activities that affect their growth in that area. If they are not ready for an activity—for example, if they recognize that they cannot yet balance on a 3-inch beam or feel comfortable in a large group of older children—they will avoid those pursuits if the environment permits.

They also agree that the development of "the whole child" is necessary; that is, not only the child's physical growth but also emotional, social, and intellectual development are important. The notion that play is only exercise of the body is incorrect. Children have many developmental needs other than physical development that are satisfied by play. They may also develop a sense of security, confidence, and safety; a feeling of being loved; strong relationships with other human beings; and a sense of independence and of initiative; as well as many other emotional, social, and intellectual accomplishments.

It has been determined that certain activities found in a social or play setting cannot usually be incorporated in a child's home. In play, as children are developing individually, they are also learning to relate to a group, to interact and "fit in." They learn to share space and materials and to await their turns in doing things. Naturally, these situations create conflicts within the individual child, as well as among children, and give rise to aggression and other feelings that the child must learn to control. Thus, personal development and social development or adaptation can often occur simultaneously.

Research has also indicated that the physical and social environments directly influence a child's development and that a stimulating, rich, and varied environment is essential in enabling the child to reach his or her greatest potential. The growing child is developing characteristics that are most susceptible to environmental influence, so it is vital that any setting designed for children's use—whether a day-care center, schoolroom, or playground—provide as much stimulation as possible.

It has recently become clear that malnourishment of children can affect them into adulthood. The dangerous results of nutritional or emotional malnourishment are unquestioned. But children can also be socially and intellectually malnourished. The lack of such stimulation at an early age as a result of boring and unvaried experiences in a sterile milieu has a harmful effect on children's further development. This is perhaps most important for preschool and elementary school children. Any environment designed for children's play or learning should provide not only different kinds of experiences, but should also stimulate the child to explore and manipulate that environment.

DEVELOPMENTAL NEEDS

In designing an environment for children's play, the architect or landscape architect should take the aforementioned principles of growth and development into account. By offering a variety of activity settings, the planned environment can arouse the child's interest, allow exploration and development at the child's own pace, and stimulate the child in various ways simultaneously. It will then be a positive influence on the growth and development of the child. Such an environment should provide all of the following kinds of stimulation.

Physical stimulation should be of two kinds, sensory and motor. Sensory stimulation includes impressions received through the senses—touching and being touched, seeing colors and forms, hearing sounds. All development begins with sensory response; an environment rich in sights and sounds will contribute immensely to the child's development. Equally important is motor stimulation, which includes large and small muscle play and activities that support eye-hand, eye-foot coordination. Research shows that the more physical activities children are allowed to experience—that is, the more objects they handle, the more running, climbing, crawling, and balancing they do—the healthier, livelier, and happier they will be. Their development will be accelerated, and thus they will be more likely to reach their fullest potentials. Children have a great need for motor activity; therefore any setting for play and learning should provide plenty of space and equipment to accommodate this need.

The need for *perceptual stimulation* is connected with the need for sensory and motor stimulation. To perceive is to put stimuli in order and to learn to recognize patterns, such as the recurrence of a familiar street or the repetition of sounds as rhythm and music. Perceptions about sensory and motor experiences will increase as children experiment with and repeat activities. Perceptual development also comes from emotional, social, and intellectual experiences, for we develop perceptions about all aspects of life. Thus, experiences that stimulate perceptual growth are needed in any environment for children. Activities that develop representational skills—building with sand, playing make-believe on a treehouse "stage," and role playing—all provide perceptual experience.

Experiences that develop children's abilities to understand and control their emotions are as important as those that affect physical and perceptual growth. *Emotional stimulation* is essential to improve a child's ability to deal with difficult or stressful situations. Children must actually experience emotions in order to develop them within themselves. They must know the joy and terror of swinging high, the anger of being shoved out of line, the satisfaction of exploring on a nature walk. Children's feelings of being liked and trusted, their sense of sympathy for others, their ability to channel destructive impulses into constructive energy—to talk instead of hit—are all affected by the environment.

Social development requires that children learn to relate to and interact with other people and to adapt their egocentric views of the world to include other children and adults. The importance of *social stimulation* in a child's development is clear; socialization is at the core of the learning process. It means trying on self-images, connecting with peers, and working out human relationships. Socializing is part of the process by which we acquire the resources for growing up.

Recent research has strongly suggested that an important factor in social growth is mixing children of different ages, not segregating younger children from older children as in the past. While children of different ages may have different levels of physical development, it is important that their environments provide areas of interaction. Young children find it extremely stimulating to be with older children, who provide role models for growth and accelerate their development. The social development of older children is also enhanced by learning to care for and understand small children.

Finally, *intellectual stimulation* is as important in the play setting as in the classroom. Activities that are important for the development of intelligence are: exploring, working on one's own, communicating, using new materials, fantasizing, and undergoing new experiences. Intellectually stimulating activities are those that encourage children to be curious and to wonder; to investigate independently what things are, how they function, and how they relate to one another; to solve problems and understand situations with others; and to express ideas and feelings in language. The puzzle of a maze, the wonder of growing plants, and the rules of a game are all intellectually stimulating. Thus, activities that encourage intellectual growth occur on the playground as well as in the classroom.

PLAY AND LEARNING

The general theories of learning and development discussed above may seem to have little to do with playground design. Yet the principles apply as much to play as to other childhood activities, for play is an important, even necessary, part of a child's growth and development. Play is one of the ways children learn. The setting provided for play—ideally, a varied and stimulating playscape—should provide opportunities for that growth and development.

Plato is often cited as the first to recognize the practical value of play because of the prescriptions in his "Laws" to distribute apples among boys to help them learn arithmetic and to give real miniature tools to those three-year-olds who were later to become builders. Following the ideas of the great educational reformers of the seventeenth and eighteenth centuries—Rousseau, Pestalozzi, and Froebel—teachers increasingly accepted the idea that education should take into account the child's natural interests and stages of development. Friedrich Froebel's stress on the importance of play in learning was of central interest. He realized that the kind of play children enjoy and the toys that attract them most could be used to increase their attention span and to develop their learning capacities.

The first complete formulations of theories of play came in the mid- to late-nineteenth century, under the influence of evolutionary theory. Several theories of play that date back to the last century, now known as "classical theories," express ideas that are still widely accepted, especially among the general public. These include, among others:

Surplus energy: organisms indulge in play to release surplus energy or surplus vitality.

Instinct: human play is an instinct retained from our animal ancestors who, perhaps for physical conditioning, indulged in vigorous, repeated, often spectacular exercises.

Preparation: children's play is preparation for adult work and living; through imitation and fantasy play, for example, the child learns how to be an adult.

Relaxation: play is a recuperation or restoration from work; play is not serious but only an escape from earning a living.

These classical theories of play all have certain limitations that make it impossible for contemporary educators and psychologists to be content with them. The classical theories try to find a single function for all kinds of play. However, it is far more likely that play consists of a great diversity of activities that do not all serve the same purpose. Even a single form of play may fulfill several different needs.

Above all, however, it should be recognized that play is an earnest as well as an enjoyable activity, that it is not simply an interlude in human behavior, a dispensible if refreshing indulgence. It is, rather, a vitally important activity of human life that, in fact, exists among the members of all human societies at all ages.

Developmental Stages of Play

Twentieth-century theorists have provided more useful analyses of play. The work of Jean Piaget represents the kind of helpful understanding and practical model that can be derived if the study of early growth and development is pursued. In fact, some of the following material about forms of play is not Piaget's alone, but a combination of the work of several theorists and researchers.

Jean Piaget emphasizes the interrelationship of the individual and his or her environment and the vital role it plays in the development of intellect in children. He sees intelligence as a special form of adaptation that consists of a continuous, creative interaction between the organism and the environment. Piaget divided the growth of children—starting with the instinctual responses of infancy and leading to the eventual achievement of logical adult thinking—into various stages, each with its own characteristic form of play.

For example, Piaget calls the period from birth to eighteen to twenty-four months of age the *sensorimotor phase*, a stage in which the child moves from the passive responses of infancy to such active responses as searching for objects, demanding food, expressing anger, and so forth. Children of this age learn to coordinate separate activities—to follow the motion of their hands with their eyes and to control that motion; to look for things that have been removed from their field of vision; to be aware of depth and space and to maneuver in the space; to observe the actions of others and to imitate them. The sensorimotor phase is marked by functional or practice play in the form of repetitious actions. Constant repetition, such as picking up and dropping an object over and over, is a process that takes place with a great sense of urgency and concentration. Children gain pleasure from being able to control themselves and their environment to some extent.

Genuine *constructive play* emerges around twenty-two to twenty-four months of age. Children begin to play with a purpose; their activity results in creating and in the ability to use play materials to fulfill a purpose. Play is sustained over longer periods of time, and children eventually begin to cooperate with their peers in constructive play.

At the age of two or three, children use more complex materials, since they are engaged in constructive and low-order *symbolic play*. Symbolic play is associated with the *preconceptual phase*—from eighteen to twenty-four months to four years—during which children develop the ability to create symbols, imitate the actions of others, and learn language. Symbolic play gives children a way to assimilate their new skills of representing or symbolizing objects and events. Prevalent forms of symbolic play are pretending and imitating.

Until about the age of four, children are so involved with themselves that little attention is available for the activities of other children. They may play together, but their play is primarily individual. They do, however, enjoy the presence of other children in parallel play, where each child is immersed in his or her own world, only occasionally interacting with others. Four- and five-year-old children are more social, and their play materials are more varied and complex. They make greater use of the playground—stacking, building, and climbing.

The highest form of symbolic play is *sociodramatic play*. When children pretend or take on the roles of someone else by imitating actions and speech they are engaging in dramatic play; when this imitation is carried on with another role-player, the play becomes sociodramatic.

The *intuitive phase*, from four years to seven or eight years, is marked by children's increasing ability to conceptualize and to organize their experience into increasingly logical concepts. Children use their intuitions and are continually attempting to make their intuitions correspond to reality. This is thus the stage of incessant questioning. Their social world also begins to grow, as they become more aware of other children and strive to imitate their activities. During the primary years of school, children expand constructive and sociodramatic play into full-fledged games with rules, and the individual child learns to adjust his or her behavior to the rules of the game. Rules may also be present in sociodramatic play, but they are imposed by the standards of life. However, games with imposed rules are more competitive and demand a minimum of verbalization. By the age of seven, children have adopted games with rules as the predominant form of play; this form continues into adulthood. In this phase, however, the rules are not perfectly understood and are subject to individual interpretations.

The *concrete operations phase* occurs from seven to eight and continues to eleven to twelve. Thought becomes more detached from perception or action, and children are better able to organize experience into categories such as class, relation, and number. Children enter into more complex social relations and have intense interest in playing games with rules. They develop the ability to work with others toward a common goal, making team efforts possible. They also become interested in the world of concrete objects and events; they want to see, smell, and touch on a first-hand basis.

The final stage of childhood development is the *formal operations phase*, which begins at eleven to twelve and continues to fifteen or sixteen. Adult thought processes begin during adolescence. Children of this age can deal with the form of an argument without necessarily being concerned with its content; they can formulate theories and hypotheses that can be tested against reality. In terms of play, adolescents remain preoccupied with the rules of games; they delight in creating complex situations and in anticipating all the possible outcomes of a game or activity.

Piaget's theories of childhood development and play have been used here only as an example of the relevance of theory and research to the designer of play environments for children of any age. The principal point to remember is that the more varied and stimulating the activity settings are (given the restrictions of space), the more supportive a playground will be of children's growth and development.

Playground design should not be neglected because play is sometimes perceived as frivolous. Rather, the design of the play environment deserves as much consideration as the design of any living or educational environments for children. Dr. Susan Isaacs has pointed out, "Play is a child's life and the means by which he comes to understand the world he lives in." Insofar as this life and learning take place in a playground, they can be improved by making the playground into the richest and most stimulating environment possible.

Chapter 2.

A History of Playgrounds

The need for playgrounds is part of the larger need for open spaces in our cities and towns. Playgrounds are merely specialized open spaces. They are set aside and designed primarily for children's play, but they also contribute to the landscape of the city as does any other open space. Conversely, any open space is likely to be used by children for play. That we see fit to provide separate spaces for children is an acknowledgment of the needs for protection and supervision and of the encouragement of growth and learning for children.

The history of open space and its attendant recreational use is a long one, but there are some developments in the history of urban open spaces that are particularly noteworthy, at least as conceptual background for the playground designer. In classic Greek city planning, two particularly well-conceived open spaces were provided for in every town. The more well known, the *agora* ("to gather"), served as the meeting place of men, the center of village trade, and the location for the cafés. Adjacent to the *agora* was the *plateia* ("plateaued space"), which accommodated festivals, community dances, marriage celebrations, weekly parades, and, we can suppose, unsupervised children's play.

The village green in feudal times and the marketplace of the medieval town provided urban spaces for communal celebrations, similar to the plazas of South and Central American peasant villages and to the *korso* of eastern European villages today. These are all unquestionably pedestrian spaces. However, in our modern European and American cities, the great urban spaces were not primarily pedestrian but were those open areas used by carriages and other forms of transportation as well. Formal avenues with pedestrian promenades, town squares, landscaped parks, and pleasure gardens all developed as a means of maintaining order between the pedestrian and the driver.

In the nineteenth century, with the onslaught of urban housing speculation and the introduction of the industrial grid system in the rapidly growing cities, open spaces became something readily consumable. The street and the alley were the only remaining amenities, at least for the lower-income classes. The alley became the retreat from the tenement, and the street was the communal meeting place. As Lewis Mumford aptly puts it in *The City in History*:

> The street was forced to take the place of the back garden and protected square of the medieval town, or of the open place and park of the baroque order. Thus this paved desert, adapted primarily to wheeled traffic, became also park, promenade, and playground; a grim park, a dusty promenade, a dangerous playground.[1]

The recent development of playgrounds is a result of the important search for more and better open spaces in our cities and towns. Areas set aside for children's play simply did not exist before the end of the nineteenth century, except perhaps for the children of the very rich. According to Mumford, "No serious public recognition of the need for children's playgrounds came until after 1870."[2] The reasons for this late development of playgrounds lie in our historical attitudes toward children and the changing social and educational conditions of the time.

Historians such as J.H. Plumb have discovered that children were not thought of as individuals different from adults until rather recently. "The world that we think proper to children—fairy stories, games, toys, special books for learning, even the idea of childhood itself—is a European invention of the past four hundred years."[3] Until the nineteenth century there was no separate world of childhood for most children. They performed their part in providing for the family by working in the home or perhaps on a farm or in a factory, and they were expected to play—if they were allowed free time at all—in the farmyard or streets and parks of the town.

Gradually, however, children were separated from the adult world as a result of a combination of social changes: the passage of child labor laws; the growth of public education, with the later extension of the school year from four or five months to nine months; and the increasing prosperity of the middle and lower classes in the nineteenth century. Instead of working for wages, children were given the "job" of getting an education. Eventually, they were given more of the leisure time that today is a privilege of attending school, including that period called recess, the after-school hours before dinner, and those long, glorious vacations that adults often envy. Thus, the need for a place for children to play developed only *after* the freeing of children from labor.

THE FIRST PLAYGROUNDS IN AMERICA

Although such spaces as the common in Boston are often cited as early evidence of an awareness of children's need for spaces to play (even though the common also provided pasturage for cows), the first *organized* playgrounds in the United States were not established until the 1880s and 1890s. They were created primarily by philanthropic organizations concerned with getting slum children off the streets, where horse and trolley traffic presented both health and bodily dangers.

Although temporary vacation school playgrounds existed earlier, the modern playground movement in America seems to have begun with the *sand garden*, which consisted of a large sandbox made of wood, placed in the Parmenter Street Chapel and West End Nursery in Boston in 1885. The work was done by the Massachusetts Emergency and Hygiene Association at the suggestion of Dr. Marie Zakrzewska, who had seen sand gardens and boxes in Berlin, Germany. Within two years ten sand gardens had been built in Boston, mostly in the courts of tenement buildings; by 1899 the association sponsored twenty-one such playgrounds.

Early sand garden in Boston. From Clarence E. Rainwater, The Play Movement in the United States, *p. 22.*

Similar playgrounds were created in other cities before the end of the century. In 1891 the New York Society of Parks and Playgrounds opened its first playgrounds on the Upper East Side. They were equipped with sandpiles, small wagons, wheelbarrows, shovels, and also with swings, see-saws, footballs, and other equipment. Charitable groups established play-grounds in Philadelphia in 1893, in Chicago in 1894, and in Detroit in 1899. By 1900, there were also playgrounds in Providence, Pittsburgh, Brooklyn, Baltimore, Milwaukee, Cleveland, Minneapolis, and Denver.

These early playgrounds had several common characteristics. They were for the use of young children; they were located in the densely populated sections of cities; they received funding from philanthropic sources; they were maintained only during the summer vacation period; and they contained equipment that was suitable only for outdoor use. These playgrounds combined ball-playing areas with areas of fixed equipment as did the traditional playground, which was hard-surfaced, bleak, and furnished with commercially manufactured equipment for physical exercise.

The first playground that represented a step forward in design was the so-called model playground at Jane Addams's Hull House in Chicago, set up in 1894. It too had a charitable purpose, that of combatting juvenile delinquency. As Jane Addams said, "Every city in the United States spends a hundred fold more money for juvenile reform than is spent providing means for public recreation, and none of us, as yet, sees the folly and shame of such procedure."[4] She also asserted that "amusement is stronger than vice "[5] as support for playgrounds. Planners of the Hull House playground sought to determine what specific apparatuses, activities, and supervision would best attract and guide children.

Other model playgrounds were built in Philadelphia, Providence, New York, and Boston before 1900. These playgrounds were somewhat experimental in nature but were based on the recognition that play had educational as well as recreational value, that older as well as young children should be served, and that the playground should be open year-round.

A third kind of playground developed before 1900 was the large recreational park, or outdoor gymnasium. The first was the Charlesbank Playground in Boston, proposed by the Massachusetts Emergency and Hygiene Association in 1886 and funded in part by the Boston Park Department. Designed by Frederik Law Olmstead, it was built from 1889–91 and provided recreation areas for adults as well as children. It contained an open-air gymnasium with a running track for men at one end; an interior park that had the usual landscape features of other city parks; and a gymnasium for women and a playground for children at the other end. Charlesbank had buildings equipped with all kinds of gymnastic apparatus, locker rooms, and a paid instructor. Similar recreation parks were built in Louisville, Philadelphia, New York, and Chicago by 1900.

MUNICIPAL AND SCHOOL PLAYGROUNDS

The second stage of the playground movement in America began with the financial involvement of municipal and educational agencies. There was some early opposition to public funding: playgrounds were called "the fads of women," and one opponent said, "I would vote $1,200 for workground, but never one cent for idle play."[6] However, many communities readily voted such sums of money for municipal or school playgrounds.

The most important early municipal playground system was the South Park Playgrounds begun in Chicago in 1903. Almost certainly modeled after Charlesbank in Boston, this group of ten parks provided both indoor and outdoor facilities for public use. The parks were open day and evening year-round and were equipped with two trained instructors—a man and a woman—per park. These parks enclosed ten to sixty acres and contained athletic and ball fields (flooded for ice-skating in winter), outdoor gymnasiums, playgrounds for small children, swimming pools, field houses (de-

Plan of Charlesbank Playground in Boston by Frederik Law Olmstead. From Arthur Leland and Lorna Higbee Leland, Playground Technique and Playcraft, *p. 59.*

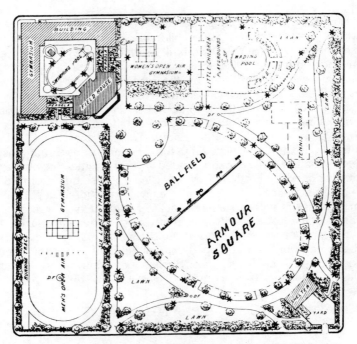

Plan of Armour Square, Chicago Parks System. From Arthur Leland and Lorna Higbee Leland, Playground Technique and Playcraft, *p. 77.*

signed by Daniel Burnham), and auditorium and club rooms. The Chicago system was imitated on a smaller scale in Los Angeles beginning in 1905; by 1912, Pittsburgh, Philadelphia, Minneapolis, St. Paul, Oakland, and Louisville had also opened public field houses and parks.

About the same time municipal playgrounds were developed, public funding for school playgrounds also began, first in Philadelphia in 1896. In 1898 New York opened thirty-one playgrounds under the auspices of the Board of Education, and other cities soon followed this trend. The number of school playgrounds around the country increased dramatically in the next decade for two reasons: the institution of play and athletics into the school curriculum, and the attempt to avoid redundant spending by combining community and school facilities.

Playtime and physical exercise were incorporated into the school curriculum most fully in Gary, Indiana, where an attempt was made to adopt the ideas of Friedrich Froebel for both elementary and high school children. This plan, known eventually as the Gary plan, required large school sites, from ten to twenty acres, containing not only playgrounds, but also park features for the public, school gardens, and athletic fields. The school day was extended to accommodate the required physical education programs, and one-quarter of the teachers hired were physical "trainers." Elementary school children had two hours a day of organized play (in addition to recess); high school students had one hour a day. Froebel felt that mind

and soul are expressed through bodily activity and expression, and emphasized the importance of activity settings—especially areas for playing ball,
which he considered a very important physical activity—in supporting this
growth.

Eventually, the inclusion of physical education classes in the school
curriculum spread to other schools—for example to New York on a test
basis in 1914 and on a general basis in 1915. The incorporation of play
into a gym period had become fairly standard by the 1920s and, of course,
continues today. The primary problem in adopting the Gary plan, however,
was the inadequate size of most city school sites.

School playgrounds were also developed to avoid spending money on
both municipal and educational sites. The most significant connection of
municipal and school facilities came in the use of existing school buildings
as community recreation centers. New York City first used schools for this
purpose in 1898, but Rochester, New York, attracted national attention in
1907 by using schoolhouses to eliminate the cost of constructing field
houses. Other cities followed this example, with Milwaukee achieving special recognition as "the city of the lighted schoolhouses."

President Theodore Roosevelt significantly influenced the growth of
municipal and school playgrounds. His interest in physical fitness and exercise gave the entire playground movement considerable publicity. He declared that there could be no more important reform than to provide
adequate playgrounds and in so doing probably influenced many cities to
provide the necessary funds.

Even more impetus for the development of municipal and school playgrounds came from the Playground Association of America, founded in
1906 when only twenty or so cities had playgrounds. Ten years later, 500
to 600 cities had recreational facilities. The association named President
Roosevelt as its honorary president, but the driving force behind the movement was a group of early promoters of playgrounds including: Dr. Luther
Gulick, city supervisor of physical education in New York City; Dr. Henry
Curtis, a playground director in Washington, D.C.; and Joseph Lee, a phi-
lanthropist and pioneer social worker. The association began publishing a
magazine, The Playground, in 1907; and an outline for the comprehensive
training of recreation workers was published in 1910, entitled Normal
Course in Play. In addition to such educational activities, efforts were made
to develop playground legislation. In 1908 the Massachusetts Playground
Referendum for Cities and Towns of over Ten Thousand Inhabitants supported the need for playgrounds. In 1917 Dr. Henry Curtis, in his history of
the association, The Play Movement and Its Significance, proposed an
outline for an ideal playground law. He wanted to ensure school playground spaces of three acres for elementary schools and six acres for high
schools; to require five hours of play and physical training a week (beyond
the recess period) for both elementary and high school students; to provide
funds for schools hiring qualified directors of play and physical training for
after-school, Saturday, and summer hours; and to include an office of
Commissioner of Recreation in a state's Board of Education.

In 1911 the association changed its name to The Playground and
Recreation Association of America. This change indicated a shift in concern.

Originally, playgrounds, sponsored by charitable organizations, were for slum children; the focus changed to recreational facilities for all levels of society at all ages sponsored by cities and schools. In 1930 the association changed its name again, to the National Recreation Association, indicating that the specific concern for children's playgrounds had become much less important. In fact, in the previous ten years, the chief concern of the association had been to establish public recreation facilities throughout the nation. The association could boast that 700 cities had recreation facilities administered by some department of the local government; that 137 colleges and universities had training courses for leaders in recreation and physical education; that the number of employed recreation leaders doubled; and that spending for recreation had jumped nearly fivefold.

In schools as well, the emphasis gradually changed from free forms of play to more structured physical exercise programs. Gymnastics was introduced into American schools as early as 1823 at the Round Hill School in Massachusetts. In 1860 the YMCA was founded to promote athletics and gymnastics as safeguards against vice in young men. At about the same time, the health of women and girls was strongly promoted by Dio Lewis (*New Gymnastics for Men, Women and Children*, 1862). The American Association for Health, Physical Education and Recreation was founded in 1885, and in 1892 Ohio became the first state to make gymnastics and physical education compulsory in public schools. With the coming of World War I, the country became even more conscious of the fitness of its youth and, as a result, physical exercise and, later, competitive sports received much more emphasis in school programs than other forms of play such as manipulative, fantasy, and quiet play. With the increasing passion for organized play and athletic games, the school playground became, in reality, an outdoor gymnasium.

PLAYGROUND SITES AND EQUIPMENT

Many characteristics of the playgrounds developed early in this century are still with us. A look at photographs of playground equipment in 1908 reveals equipment much like that used on traditional playgrounds today—swings, slides, seesaws, giant strides, and so forth. The fixed equipment recommended for a small or rural playground was limited to a sand bin for smaller children, as well as swings, horizontal bars, a jumping track, and seesaws. Such standardized equipment quickly became popular because it allowed more children to play in a smaller space and because it could be easily ordered from a catalog by a local school board that did not want to pay for a designer or that did not wish to explore more creative forms of play. The desire was often for inexpensive, easily maintained apparatus that could be used by the children without much supervision.

Whether such equipment had any value beyond providing physical exercise was not known, nor were there established safety and construction standards for the usual playground apparatus. In 1917, when the playground movement was well underway, Dr. Henry Curtis still questioned the value of swings and the seesaw:

Swings at the Violet Street Playground in Los Angeles. From Arthur Leland and Lorna Higbee Leland, Playground Technique and Playcraft, *p. 156.*

> We do not know what apparatus gives as definite training and what apparatus is only a decoration, an advertisement, or a mental dissipation. Psychologically the use and effect of some apparatus is similar to getting drunk . . . . Take the simplest piece, the seesaw. Has it any value? If so, what is it? Apparently it has little physical value, little social value, no direct moral value. What value it has seems to come from a certain emotional excitement that accompanies it.[7]

Some observers thought that the effect of using swings was similar either to a drowsy self-hypnosis or the pleasure of foreign travel.

Other elements of playground construction—location, size, site, and supervision—were generally agreed upon, although they differed from today's standards. It was recommended that playgrounds be within a quarter of a mile from every home with children under ten; that an acre of ground be provided for every 1000 to 1500 children (similar to the rule of the Board of Education for London schools in England of 30 square feet per child); that the principal site requirement was level ground (for the large ball fields or running tracks); and that supervision was necessary because "it goes without a challenge that play must be supervised, that the child does not know how to play."[8]

As the traditional playground developed into a flat, hard-surfaced area with isolated sets of equipment, the voices of those writers who recommended a variety of play settings or equipment were not heard. For example, in 1908, Dr. Joseph Lee, in his book *Play and Playgrounds*, offered many intelligent suggestions. For children under six, he suggested that the playground should provide workable materials such as sand, blocks, paper, and clay; movable things, such as toys; props and places for dramatic play; and areas for social activities, such as circle games. Furthermore, all of these play activities should occur during regular playtimes for children in the neighborhood. For children from six to eleven—which Dr. Lee called the

Big Injun stage, characterized by a desire for reality, a love of mischief, and a natural interest in experimentation—he recommended such things as *Country in the Town* (that is, landscaping with trees, grass, and so forth), nature study, nurturing of animals, care of gardens, sloyd (or woodworking), contests, and quiet games, all under the direction of instructors. He also suggested that a playground should accommodate different age groups, be used in all seasons (that is, provide an area for flooding in the winter to allow ice-skating and hockey), and be open after school, evenings, Saturdays, and summers with the instructors present at these hours as well as during school hours. Dr. Lee's recommendations seem more descriptive of the modern playscape than the playground as it was developing early in this century. Early recommendations for playground surfaces were not always for the hard surfaces, such as asphalt, that eventually became standard. Arthur Leland and Lorna Higbee Leland, who constructed playgrounds in St. Paul, recommended soft sand under seesaws and climbing bars, with soft areas to land on under swings and giant strides as well. Grass as a surface for games was recommended if it could be well maintained.

Finally, the involvement of children in constructive play—including the building of the playground—was occasionally urged, though all too often ignored. As the Lelands wrote:

> When we give the child ready-made things, ready-made toys, ready-made playground apparatus, ready-made playgrounds, which he could make himself and in so doing receive valuable training we give him stones instead of bread.[9]

Despite these early voices recommending the employment of paid instructors and a variety of environments and activities in playgrounds, the trend continued toward standardized equipment, hard and flat surfaces, and easy, inexpensive maintenance. These playgrounds are still with us everywhere, even though they are dangerous and ignore many aspects of a child's learning and development. The result, as reported in the last two decades, has been an appalling number of playground accidents resulting primarily from falls onto hard-packed earth, asphalt, or concrete, or from poor design or hazardous features of manufactured equipment.

The traditional playgrounds that still exist are far too hazardous. Reports from such sources as the U.S. Consumer Product Safety Commission (1975), the National Recreation and Parks Association (1975), and the National Electronic Injury Surveillance System record hundreds of thousands of injuries a year. And these injuries are much worse than cuts and bruises, they often require treatment in hospital emergency rooms and include fractured skulls, hangings, amputations, and so forth. Despite these reports; however, tens of thousands of playgrounds remain in use with antiquated equipment installed on hard surfaces.

In the late 1970s, the U.S. Consumer Product Safety Commission issued guidelines for playground design, surfacing, and equipment. The commission concluded that the guidelines would not be mandatory because

> [such a] specification rule by itself would not adequately address the problem of playground injuries. Such factors as the diverse ways equipment is used, the varying quality of supervision on equipment, equipment placement, and equipment maintenance all play a part in playground injuries.[10]

Because seven out of ten serious injuries incurred on playgrounds are the result of falls, the most important recommendations of the commission concerned the playground's surfacing material. The commission found that "concrete, asphalt, and similar materials are not recommended for use under playground equipment because of their hard, unyielding characteristics." Instead, loose materials—both organic, such as bark or mulch, and inorganic, such as sand—provide the safest surface when applied to a depth of at least six inches. Although sand and other loose materials require regular maintenance for smoothing and replacement, the advantages they have over asphalt or even compact materials, such as outdoor rubber mats, justify the added care and expense. Concerning playground organization, the commission recommended that the equipment's "use zone"—the largest arc of a swing including a child's extended legs, for instance—should be considered in the planning process. It was also determined that buildings, paths, and other play areas should be at least eight feet from the estimated use zone of a piece of equipment.

PLAYGROUND PLANNING IN EUROPE

Playgrounds developed in Europe at about the same time as in the United States, and in some ways resembled the traditional American playground. They had gravel surfaces, but trees and shrubs were planted on the edges. In some cases they were without equipment and thus provided no more than open space for running and ball games. When equipment was added, it was the standardized playground apparatus of swings, seesaws, and so forth. The notion that play is not serious but rather a form of amusement was evident in the equipment that copied structures in amusement parks, such as the carousel.

Some equipment—especially the parallel bars and horizontal bars that were later incorporated into extensive systems—was created as a result of the gymnastic movement, which had been strongest in Sweden and Germany during the nineteenth century. This movement began when Johann Guts Muths—inspired by the naturalism of Rousseau's *Emile*—wrote *Gymnastics for Youth*. About the middle of the century, concerned with the physical condition of Prussia's youth for militaristic reasons, educational authorities in that country were convinced by Adolph Speiss to make physical education a part of the regular school program.

Another movement in the nineteenth century that influenced playground activities was the manual training movement. Uno Cygnaeus introduced domestic handwork—that is, woodworking, crafts, and other activities called sloyd—into Finnish schools in 1866, thereby embodying Froebel's principle of motor expression. Such handwork was demonstrated at the Centennial Exposition in 1876 in Philadelphia and led to the eventual establishment of manual training departments as well as entire schools devoted to vocational training.

In this century Denmark has been considered a leader in the development of playgrounds. Denmark was the first country to pass laws that required play facilities for children in housing projects. Denmark was also the site of the first adventure playground (see chapter 3).

As early as 1916, the Danish Sports Association (Dansk Idraets-Forbund) had published a guide for standard playgrounds called *Playgrounds: Plan, Equipment, Management, and Playleader*. Hans Draghjelm, who must also be given credit for introducing the sandbox from Germany to Denmark, wrote extensively about playgrounds in 1918, 1923, 1925, and again in 1935. The last piece, entitled, "Børnelepladsens Anlaeg, Redskaber og Drift Standardlegepladsen" (The Playground's Site—Equipment and Maintenance), elaborated on and altered some of what was in the 1918 playground guide. Draghjelm suggested that the playground be set on a dry and sunny site, and that the ground need not be flat. It could be close to a busy street as long as it was fenced off or separated from the street by shrubs. He emphasized the importance of green areas and landscaping. In addition, he felt that the playground should not be more than a ten- to fifteen-minute walk from the users' homes; thus several small playgrounds, rather than one large one, were preferable in a town or city because more children would have access to them. A concern for playgrounds for different age groups was indicated in 1923 when a government publication dealt with the differences between playgrounds for small children and sports areas for older children.

In 1939 Denmark began legislation to control the development of playgrounds. On March 29, 1939, a building law was instituted in Copenhagen that required apartment buildings housing more than eight families to provide a playground for children, designed to fit within the possibilities of the site. In effect, this provided play areas for preschool children that were close to the entrance of the complex. The problem of providing play areas for older children after school and on weekends was not addressed by this law. More recent building laws for all of Denmark, also adapted and passed by other European countries, have made the 1939 law stronger and expanded the concept. A 1967 law lessened the suggested walking distance between playgrounds, from ten to fifteen minutes in 1939 to only five minutes in 1967. The basic effect of this law was to require more playgrounds than ever before.

NOTES

1. Lewis Mumford, *The City in History: Its Origins, Its Transformations, and Its Prospects* (New York: Harcourt, Brace, and World, Inc., 1961), p. 427.

2. Ibid., pp. 426–27.

3. J.H. Plumb, "The Great Change in Children," *Horizon* 13, no. 1 (Winter 1971): p. 6.

4. Quoted by Joseph Lee in a pamphlet promoting the *Massachusetts Playground Referendum*, Massachusetts Civic League, 1908.

5. Arthur Leland and Lorna Higbee Leland, *Playground Technique and Playcraft*, Vol. 1, 2d ed., (New York: Doubleday Page and Co., 1913), p. 37.

6. Deobold B. Van Dolen, Elmer D. Mitchell, and Bruce L. Bennett, *A World*

History of Physical Education: Cultural, Philosophical, Comparative (New York: Prentice-Hall, Inc., 1953), p. 406.

7. Henry Curtis, *The Play Movement and Its Significance* (New York: Macmillan Co., 1917), p. 19.

8. Harold D. Meyer, "The Rural Playground" *University of North Carolina Extension Bulletin* 1, no 6: p. 7.

9. Leland and Leland, *Playground Technique*, p. 161.

10. U.S. Consumer Product Safety Commission, *A Handbook for Public Playgrounds*; vol. 1, *General Guidelines for New and Existing Playgrounds* (Washington, D.C.; U.S. Government Printing Office, 1981), p. 11.

Chapter 3.
The Adventure Playground

The adventure playground—also known as the junk playground, workyard, or Robinson Crusoe playground—is the most significant development in playground design in the last forty years. It represents a real change from the traditional playground concept.

The adventure playground is not based on the use of manufactured, exercise-oriented equipment set in a planned environment. Instead, loose materials are provided—usually discarded lumber, tires, pipes, bricks, and other "junk"—which children can freely manipulate. The children can alter the playground environment as they wish by building, digging, and demolishing. Under the supervision of a play leader, who shows children how to use the tools and conducts other activities, the children follow their own day-to-day interests, sometimes involving themselves in construction projects that take many weeks.

The first adventure playground—in Danish, *skrammellegeplads* or *byggeplads*—was built in 1943 in Copenhagen. It was the result of an earlier observation by the landscape architect C. Th. Sørensen. He had noticed children playing happily on a construction site, using the tools and materials they found laying about while ignoring organized playgrounds nearby. In his 1931 book *Parkpolitik i Sogn og Købstad (Open Spaces for Town and Country)*, he wrote: "Perhaps we should try to set up waste material playgrounds in suitable large areas where children would be able to play with old cars, boxes, and timber."

In 1943, during the German occupation, the Workers Cooperative Housing Association (Arbejdernes Andelsboligforenings Bebyggelse) in Emdrup built a large playground on the site of a housing development. The architect, Dan Fink, worked with Sørensen himself. Children were given large amounts of discarded building materials and other so-called *skrammel*, or junk, to create their own playground. The playground consisted of 6,000 square meters covered with grass and surrounded by two-meter-high earth banks that were planted with shrubs and flowers on the sides facing the apartment buildings. There was only one entrance to the playground, primarily for security reasons. A minimum number of permanent buildings were provided— including a play hut for inclement weather, toilets, storage space, and an office for the play leader—as well as a large supply of discarded material for adventurous play. For the first fourteen years, the

The first adventure playground, 1943, C. Th. Sørensen, Emdrup. (SBBU, Socialt Boligbyggeris Ungdomsklubber)

playground was open during the summer only. It still exists but has now become a self-governing institution and is open year-round.

The adventure playground in Emdrup aroused interest outside of Denmark. In 1946 it was visited by Lady Marjorie Allen of Hurtwood, an English landscape gardener, who returned to London to organize such playgrounds there. Lady Allen wrote:

> When I worked among children condemned to live in barbaric and subhuman surroundings, my thoughts always returned to my early good fortune [of growing up in a rural setting]. The remembrance has made me more determined than ever to restore to these children some part of their lost childhood; gardens where they can keep their pets and enjoy their hobbies and perhaps watch their fathers working with real tools; secret places where they can create their own worlds; the shadow and mystery that lend enchantment to play.[1]

The first English adventure playground was established in 1948 in Camberwell, London. More playgrounds followed in other parts of London as well as in Liverpool, Bristol, and some of the "new towns." By 1962, the London Adventure Playground Association was established to provide new playgrounds with information concerning such matters as site, fencing, materials, supervision, and insurance.

The Emdrup project also inspired the first Swiss adventure playground, the Robinson Crusoe playground, built in 1954 by the architect Alfred Trachsel in Zürich. It offered zones for many activities, including building,

*An adventure playground today.
(SBBU, Socialt Boligbyggeris Ungdomsklubber)*

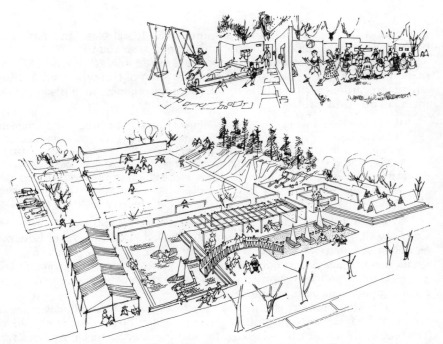

*Robinson Crusoe Playground, Zürich. Designed by Alfred Trachsel. From
Alfred Ledermann and Alfred Trachsel,* Spielplatz und Gemeinschaftszentrum, *p. 129.*

theatrical performances, care of animals, gardening, sand and water play, and so forth. Leaders were regarded as necessary for large playgrounds such as this one.

Since the 1950s, adventure playgrounds have spread throughout Europe, especially in England, Denmark (which now has more than twenty), and Sweden (where the first was called Freetown in Stockholm). One reason for this growth is that the basic concept of the adventure playground—that of giving back to urban children opportunities for free and creative play—coincided with the need for repair of war damage in many European cities. As a result, many bombed sites were used for playgrounds, and the need for play areas for children was considered in the planning of new housing and towns.

THE ADVENTURE PLAYGROUND CONCEPT

The adventure playground seeks to provide certain elements of rural play to the urban child. It is argued by adventure playground supporters such as Arvid Bengtsson, former president of the International Playground Association, that in cities of fifty or one hundred years ago space and materials for creative play were abundant. Opportunities existed to play with such natural elements as earth, sand, water, fire, and plants, and to build with such intriguing junk as discarded wood, pipe, bricks, and so forth. However, these opportunities do not generally exist for today's urban children. The reasons for this are many. As Mr. Bengtsson puts it:

> Fifty years ago, one had a pedestrian community of all ages living and working together in a wholly accessible area—a complete environment with no segregation. [However] modern residential areas are dominated by the car. A child playing is a nuisance. The street can no longer be a playground and modern courtyards are generally just ornamental. A little playground tucked away in a corner seldom relates to the number of potential users.[2]

Although Bengtsson perhaps overstates the case (photographs of street scenes fifty years ago show the same traffic problems we have today, whether horsedrawn or motor-driven), he is, in general, correct. Heavy traffic, lack of open spaces, life in high-rise buildings, and locked playgrounds all limit safe, creative play in the city.

The adventure playground attempts to provide a variety of play opportunities that urban children do not have. As Lady Allen wrote:

> Most young people, at one time or another, have a deep urge to experiment with earth, fire, water, and timber, to work with real tools without fear of undue criticism or censure. In these playgrounds their love of freedom to take calculated risks is recognized and can be enjoyed under tolerant and sympathetic guidance.[3]

In addition to providing opportunities for construction, most adventure playgrounds have also begun to provide places for the keeping and care of animals, from small rabbits to farmyard animals such as goats and pigs.

Playleaders and children in an adventure playground. (SBBU, Socialt Bo-ligbyggeris Ungdomsklubber)

Buildings provide year-round shelter for domestic activities such as cooking, sewing, woodworking, and so forth.

One of the most important features of the adventure playground is the play leader. However, the leader is not present to initiate or direct the play but to support it, to step in with advice and assistance only when the children ask for it, and to supervise building construction to ensure safety. Otherwise, children on adventure playgrounds are left free to pursue their own interests at their own pace. Considerable training of play leaders is necessary and it is felt that an adventure playground simply could not succeed without the friendly assistance and advice provided by such leaders. In Denmark play leaders are trained in teachers' colleges. The training program emphasizes an understanding of play and child development, and the development of arts and crafts skills and administrative techniques.

An adventure playground has thus been defined by the National Playing Fields Association of England as:

> A place where children of all ages, under friendly supervision, are free to do many things they can no longer easily do in our crowded urban society; things like building—huts, walls, forts, dens, tree houses; lighting fires and cooking; tree climbing, digging, camping; perhaps gardening and keeping animals; as well as playing team and group games, painting, dressing up, modeling, reading—or doing nothing. For it must also be a place where children just meet and talk in a free, relaxed atmosphere. They do not have to pay to enter,

nor do they join as members; they just come to the playground whenever they feel like it.[4]

ADVENTURE PLAYGROUNDS IN THE UNITED STATES

The adventure playground was first brought to the United States in 1950, when *McCall's* magazine sponsored a demonstration playground in Minneapolis, Minnesota. Supported by the local board of education, the PTA, a citizens' committee, and other volunteers, the playground known as the Yard was a highly successful, one-year experiment. However, it was not immediately copied elsewhere in the United States. In fact, it was not until the mid-1960s that other such playgrounds were built. By 1977, adventure playgrounds existed in twenty American cities in eight states; notable sites were Roxbury, Massachusetts; Eugene, Oregon; Milpitas, Irvine, and Huntington Beach, California; and Homewood, Illinois. Such larger cities as New York and Baltimore have also experimented with this form of playground.

On the whole, however, the adventure playground concept has not had strong support in the United States; nor does it seem likely to obtain it. The reason for this failure lies in the reluctance of American parents and city officials to accept certain features of the adventure playground.

Adventure playground today, with visual shielding from street. (SBBU, Socialt Boligbyggeris Ungdomsklubber)

First, one of the requirements for a successful playground is the presence of the trained play leader. The play leader's role is a vital one, not only to coordinate the materials and maintenance of the playground, but also to support the children's activities when they request help. Considerable discussion of the ideal play leader's qualities and training has taken place in Europe, and there is no doubt that this must be a paid position. The job requires long hours and skill with construction tools as well as in leading games. The play leader should not interfere with the children's play, except for safety's sake. Although recreational programs in American universities adequately train people to lead sports or crafts play, the extensive managerial, human, and engineering skills needed to become a play leader are a unique combination. The provision and training of qualified play leaders has been a major problem for adventure playgrounds in the United States, primarily because funds for the position are unavailable.

Moreover, the fact that the adventure playground is the children's domain, where they play without interference, tends to make American parents nervous. Americans sometimes seem to believe that play is frivolous, although experts have long recognized that play is serious work for a child. In addition, there is a mistaken belief that adventure playgrounds are not as safe as traditional playgrounds, that the hazards of rusty nails or collapsing structures are greater than should be allowed. The fact is, children learn to build well and safely under the guidance of the play leader. Adventure playgrounds have proven to be safer than traditional playgrounds with asphalt paving and fixed equipment.

Third, the adventure playground is admittedly unsightly. It is important for the playground to be surrounded by a visual barrier, such as a wooden fence, earth banks, or dense plantings. In fact, because the adventure playground is filled with "junk," parents of the lower socioeconomic classes regard these playgrounds as insults when placed in their neighborhoods. To these parents, it appears that the playground's builders have given them a slumlike playground rather than the "architectural" playgrounds given to other city children.

Because of these problems, the adventure playground concept, which incorporates manipulative play, has not become widely accepted and utilized in the United States. Yet the basic tenets on which the adventure playground is based offer great potential for children's learning and development. The notion of manipulative play should be incorporated into any playground design when at all possible.

NOTES

1. Colin Ward, *The Child in the City* (New York: Pantheon Books, 1978), p. 196.

2. Arvid Bengtsson, *The Child's Right to Play* (Sheffield: International Playground Association, 1974), p. 8.

3. Lady Marjorie Allen, *Planning for Play* (London: Thames and Hudson; 1968), p. 55.

4. National Playing Fields of England, "What is an Adventure Playground?" (pamphlet) n.d.

Chapter 4.

New Directions in Playground Design

Renewed attention has been given to playground design since World War II. Dissatisfaction with the traditional playground as a result of the spreading influence of the adventure playground and because play itself had become a subject of greater consideration and research generated this renewed concern. Specific reconsideration has been given to all aspects of the playground, from such narrower concerns as site, equipment, or materials, to the larger question of the design of the entire play environment.

Traditional playgrounds remain with us—in fact, they are all too plentiful—but concern for safety requirements and aesthetic appearance has led to some design improvements in manufacturered apparatus and a larger selection of surfacing materials, especially in the last ten years. However, these playgrounds remain much too dangerous to be satisfactory, and they are not equipped to satisfy the many varied developmental needs of the children who use them. Adventure playgrounds must also take into account certain important design issues—especially the means to enclose and screen from view the "unsightly" part of the playground and to provide space for tool storage.

Some new playgrounds of the past thirty years have been neither traditional nor adventure playgrounds. They reflect the influence of professional architectural and manufacturing designers. The designer's hand may be seen in a large "play sculpture" that occupies a prominent place on the site; or, the entire playground may be the work of a single architect. Being partially or totally the design of a professional, however, has not ensured the success of the play environment.

SITES

In Europe the devastation of World War II proved an unexpected benefit for children insofar as it provided an opportunity to include more and better play areas in the rebuilding plans of towns and cities. Playgrounds were included in designs for new housing developments *before* reconstruction, and the problems involved in clearing space for them among older dwellings were thus avoided.

The designer of the development was responsible for planning living quarters and parking areas, as well as play spaces. He or she had to consider the amount of open space between the buildings, the number of play areas necessary to serve the population of children, the placement of playgrounds away from traffic, and the proximity of a play area to younger and older children's homes. Although many housing authorities relied on flat, open spaces filled with conventional playground equipment to solve design problems, a few designers attempted to use new concepts.

In England, for example, Mary Mitchell used the natural contours of the land in her playground designs, constructing mounds if necessary to avoid flatness and to use as the slope for a slide. She also used tree trunks as natural climbing and viewing places.

In Switzerland, some of the most innovative designs of the 1950s were from architect Alfred Trachsel. His various creations have provided prototypes for housing development playgrounds, as well as for "multizoned play environments," which attempted to provide different kinds of play activities for children of all age groups. His playgrounds combined a variety of materials, equipment, and surfaces into different areas of play, and continue to provide inspiration for the contemporary playground designer.

The Sonnengarten playground at the Zürich-Triemli housing estate, constructed from 1951 to 1955, was exemplary. It incorporated large grass areas, a natural slope as the base for a slide, concrete ducts for crawling and climbing activities, a hard surface area for ball games, an open pavilion for sheltered seating, a natural spring flowing into a paddling pool, and a

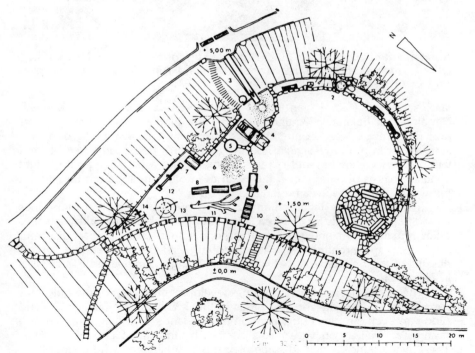

Sonnengarten Playground at Zürich-Triemli Housing Estate. Designed by Alfred Trachsel. From Alfred Ledermann and Alfred Trachsel, Spielplatz und Gemeinschaftszentrum, *p. 52.*

Sonnengarten Playground at Zürich-Triemli Housing Estate. Designed by Alfred Trachsel. From Alfred Ledermann and Alfred Trachsel, Spielplatz und Gemeinschaftszentrum, *p. 53.*

large sand area (rather than a sand pit) that served as the surface beneath climbing and balancing equipment. Only the tubular steel climbing tower and the seesaw were conventional apparatus. A similar playground for small children at the Heiligfeld housing estate provided a large belt of sand with a tree for climbing and other equipment, and a paddling pool of eight concrete basins of different heights, with the water running from the highest basin into the next lower basin, and so on.

In America the developments created by public housing authorities provided playgrounds for children living in high-rise buildings, although sites often remained flat and filled with predominantly metal play equipment. The landscape architect M. Paul Friedberg first became known for his designs of the open spaces between the buildings of the Jacob Riis Houses in New York City.

The open spaces of new housing developments were not the only sites considered appropriate for play areas in the 1950s and 1960s. In Holland Aldo van Eyck put play equipment on traffic islands, including sand pits and railings, as well as on vacant lots created by the demolition of a house. These playgrounds provided some play space for children who might otherwise have been forced to play in the streets.

"Vest-pocket" playgrounds—small, urban playgrounds build on vacant lots—developed in depressed inner-city areas in the United States in the 1960s. M. Paul Friedberg believed that creating such playgrounds could

Design of open spaces between the buildings of the Jacob Riis Houses in New York City by M. Paul Friedberg. From Richard Dattner, A.I.A., Design for Play, *p. 103.*

include neighborhood participation and that the equipment could be hand-made. Friedberg also proposed "movable" playgrounds, with prefabricated equipment that could be placed on a vacant lot for two years or so and then dismantled and moved to another lot. In this way playgrounds could be brought to neighborhoods without play or recreational areas.

The largest playgrounds developed in the twenty years after World War II were the multizoned play environments, which attempted to provide different kinds of play activities for children of all age groups. The prototype for these playgrounds was the "Robinson Crusoe" adventure playground in Zürich-Wipkingen, Switzerland, designed by Alfred Trachsel. It included an area for building activities for older children (in actuality, this was also an adventure playground) and a quiet area with a building to house a multi-purpose room for games, music, and reading; an adjacent library room; lavatories; the play leader's office; and nearby, an enclosure for theatrical and musical performances. It also included a hard surface area for street and ball games, a lawn, and a playground for smaller children, which included a hamlet of playhouses, a paddling pool with fountain, a sand pit, and other appropriate equipment. A play leader was necessary to supervise such a large site and to help children with building, gardening, theatrical, and animal-tending activities.

EQUIPMENT

Play equipment has perhaps received as much creative thinking as any other aspect of the play environment. In the 1950s, new playground equip-

Vacant lot playground in Holland by Aldo van Eyck. From Alfred Leder-mann and Alfred Trachsel, Spielplatz und Gemeinschaftszentrum, *p. 39.*

ment was created primarily in reaction against the dull colors and stark designs of traditional play apparatus. Thus, conventional swings or seesaws were sometimes merely decorated with bright colors, stripes, or the attachment of comic heads. Some equipment, however, was designed by artists— particularly pieces called "play sculptures." Designed to improve the aesthetic appearance of the playground and to stimulate children's imaginations—particularly if the sculpture was abstract and did not suggest usual play activities—play sculptures of all sizes, shapes, and materials began appearing on playgrounds throughout the world. Design competitions were sponsored by such institutions as the Corcoran Museum and the Museum of Modern Art. Individual artists who gained recognition for play sculptures included Egon Moeller Nielson of Sweden, Joseph Seebacher-Kongut of Austria, Joseph Brown of Princeton, George Huron of Hawaii, and Isamu Noguchi of Japan.

A play sculpture was often a climbing apparatus, although some combined additional play activities such as sliding and crawling. Moeller Nielson's hollow free shapes incorporated caves, ducts, and slides. Joseph Brown attempted to provide a continuous challenge to children by using unusual "unpredictable" designs. Nielson's *Prototype* and *Whale Yard* sculptures provided networks of climbing ropes that responded to the movement of children at different positions in the network.

Play equipment designed and manufactured by Kompan Multikunst, Greenwood County Day School, Midlothian, VA.

More recently, innovative manufacturers of play equipment have provided more standardized, affordable structures. Kompan of Denmark, for example, offers individual play pieces and larger structures, such as playhouses and platforms, for grouping in playgrounds. Such equipment— bright, attractive, and made with safety requirements in mind—is a significant improvement over metal, and most other currently available equipment.

One issue of debate regarding play sculptures was over the virtues of concrete versus abstract designs. If the sculpture was representative or suggestive of an animal or object, such as a horse or boat, people questioned whether the design limited the variety of play activities that could be performed with it. On the other hand, purely abstract forms may be attractive but may not suggest any uses to the children or be comfortable or easy to climb or sit on.

MATERIALS

New materials as well as new forms made from old materials began to appear on playgrounds in the 1950s and 1960s. Tubular steel, used for so long to support swings or fastened together into rectilinear monkey bars, was curved and shaped into an amazing variety of arches, circles, ladders, balancing beams, swinging towers, and so forth.

Concrete and stone became common playground equipment materials for a while, as their durability allowed easy maintenance. Concrete drums were used for tunnels and hideaways; concrete boxes became "houses"; concrete sculptures became saddle slides, turtles, or caves; and concrete or stone mounds supported slides or became "pyramids" or mountains. Entire playgrounds were sometimes constructed from cast-concrete objects, but the results were barren, uninviting, and dangerous.

Softer natural materials such as wood were occasionally seen, but their use did not increase much until the 1970s. Although wood climbing structures, peeled tree trunks, sandboxes, Wendy houses, and treehouses generally require more upkeep than concrete, if treated properly they are preferable to the harder surfaces of concrete and stone. In recent years, wooden structures have begun to replace concrete and steel constructions.

Water and sand—materials easily manipulated—are also becoming recognized as important additions to any playground. Children love to play with both water and sand, and sand has proven to be a safe surface beneath larger pieces of equipment.

THE DESIGNER'S PLAYGROUND

The creation of play sculptures eventually led to the notion of a "sculptural" or "architectural" playground. The name preferred depended on the professional training of the designer. In these playgrounds, an overall pattern of objects and equipment was created according to the aesthetic criteria of the designer. Certainly, such playgrounds were an improvement over the traditional playgrounds, which were planned without a knowledge of safety requirements. However, these playgrounds had several problems. They were often very expensive and therefore required the aid of large grants from cultural foundations or wealthy donors. They often used hard construction materials such as concrete and stone, and equipment was fixed and without moving parts. The purpose of these innovations was clearly to deter vandalism. However, because children could not manipulate their environment while playing in these areas, these playgrounds did not support their learning and development needs. Consequently, these playgrounds are all too often empty of children.

Perhaps the most successfully designed playgrounds in America during the 1960s and 1970s, comparable in approach to Alfred Trachsel's playgrounds of the 1950s, were those created by Richard Dattner. Mr. Dattner combined an awareness of the developmental needs of children with the selection of such natural materials as sand and water. One of Mr. Dattner's showcase designs was his *Adventure Playground* in Central Park, New York City, built with a grant from the Estée and Joseph Lauder Foundation. The name is misleading in that this playground in no way resembles the often haphazard jumble of wooden huts and structures found in adventure playgrounds in England, Denmark, or elsewhere in the United States. The

Plan of the playground

1 entrance	10 amphitheater
2 entrance tower	11 climbing poles
3 maze	12 slide
4 treehouses	13 volcano
5 pyramid	14 tunnel
6 splashing pool	15 concentric mounds (crater)
7 water channel	16 tree pit
8 wading pools	17 tool shed
9 table	18 boat (not installed)

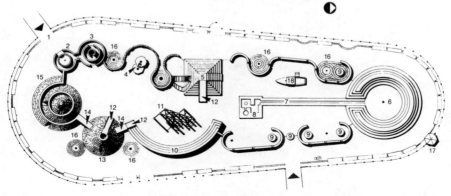

Adventure Playground in Central Park, New York City. Designed by Richard Dattner. From Richard Dattner, A.I.A., Design for Play, p. 75.

design often overuses concrete and stone, although the fact that the playground is surrounded by the expanses of grass and trees of Central Park lessens this objection. The inclusion of treehouses, a maze, splashing and wading pools connected by a water channel, safe slides, tunnels, and other equipment on a sand base all indicate Dattner's awareness of children's play needs. Playgrounds such as Dattner's represented important steps in the movement toward improving playground design.

A partial reaction to the expensive designer playground was the movement toward handmade neighborhood playgrounds that involved community members in the planning and construction processes. These playgrounds were created from discarded, surplus, or inexpensive materials. Designer Paul Hogan has been among the major proponents of such playgrounds in the 1970s. The proliferation of playgrounds using such materials as rubber tires and railroad ties brought playgrounds to many children who might not otherwise have had access to them. Paul Hogan, in his advocacy of playgrounds for free, suggested that permanent community committees be organized—each having a specific maintenance responsibility—to provide for the playground's upkeep. However, it proved easier to interest people in the short-term building project than in the long-term task of maintaining the playground.

These new directions in playground design—toward safer equipment, softer materials, and the combining of varied activity settings on a single playground—all give hope for improved playgrounds in the future. But only if all these trends are combined into a single play environment can we achieve the best playground.

Chapter 5.
School Sites as Community Parks

Both the traditional playground and the adventure playground have exhibited problems in design, in the need for play leaders, and in aesthetics, maintenance, or both. Future playgrounds should combine the successful qualities of both forms of playground. Such a playsetting—called a *playscape*—is described in chapter 6. Playscapes, however, are usually designed for younger children. A community should also consider providing new or renovated recreational environments for older children and adults. Large city and town parks are common in most urban settings, but community parks serving neighborhoods are needed now. The land need not be cleared of existing buildings in order to provide these community parks—school sites already exist for such use.

The school site that also serves as a community park can—depending upon its size—provide activity settings for all age groups. It is not a place for competitive sports, which are most effective when located on sites specifically designed for them, and, in urban settings, are shared by several schools. However, a community park located on a school site can fulfill many needs of both the neighborhood and school.

Urban communities often need parks to provide green, open spaces that relieve the confinement of repeated blocks of housing. A community park can be an amenity to any neighborhood and support individual activities as well. The development of so many vest-pocket parks in the 1970s— even though they were often poorly designed and landscaped—indicates the need for such facilities. Although urban school sites have not often been considered for development as community parks, they are ideal. Even if the school site is small—connected with a single school—it can become a neighborhood amenity and serve some of the community's as well as the school's needs. Larger school sites—in suburban or rural settings—can provide many facilities, including playscapes for very young children or for elementary and middle school children, park areas for quiet gatherings, and competitive sports fields.

Providing for the recreation needs of different age groups is not the only reason for redesigning school sites. To begin with, the sites of many elementary, middle, and high schools in the United States are unsatisfactorily designed or landscaped. All too often they resemble prison yards, enclosed as they are by cyclone fences, and invite vandalism and refuse dumping. A traditional playground may surround the school with expanses of unattractive asphalt, concrete, or bare earth; large portions of the site may be devoted to athletic fields for football or baseball with little thought given to the needs of younger children.

37

In addition, many schools and school sites are being closed and declared as surplus because of declining enrollment. Yet such schools and their sites could become real amenities to their neighborhood if thought were given to changing them into community centers and parks. A school building that provides a setting for both educational and community services might save the neighborhood school. At the same time, the school site could provide recreational facilities for the many people in the neighborhood.

This unification of school and community recreational needs presents several advantages. Multiuse facilities such as a park on the school site make the best use of available space. The school grounds can be used for extended hours, thereby making them more available to the neighborhood, less expensive to maintain because the school and park/recreation department share the cost, and less vulnerable to vandalism, especially if designed through a participatory design process. Shared sites encourage the spread of educational resources into the community—including such services as health care, day-care, after-school care for the young, senior citizen programs, vocational training, adult education, performing and creative arts programs, family and youth counseling, and municipal services. Establishing a community park on a school site satisfies the public's need and desire for nearby open spaces without redundant expenditures for separate school and public recreational facilities.

The traditional planning and design process is not suitable for creating shared sites. The traditional approach allows the clients—in this case the school and public officials—and the designer to create structures that represent their own ideas and desires rather than the ideas and desires of the users. Increasingly, however, people want a strong voice in decisions affecting their immediate environments. Without such a voice, people view their environments as impersonal, belonging to someone else, rather than identifying with them and caring about their maintenance.

It is therefore vital that the clients and designer—no matter how well intentioned—do not determine the community park's design by themselves. The users—especially the children—must participate also. It is important too that the users be genuinely involved in the design process. Attempts to do this are frequently superficial, in the form of a survey or a few questions such as "what colors would you like?" or "do you want swings?" Of course, the officials must determine general needs and budget limitations, and the designer will realize the design, mechanical, and construction problems involved; but the users know their own needs far better than the school and public officials or the designer. The best solution to any design problem is, therefore, a partnership between the users, client, and designer to create the most satisfying environment for all.

Although a community park is intended for the use of all age groups, some skepticism may be expressed at involving children in its design. It can, however, be demonstrated that children and adolescents are able to render important contributions to the design process. Indeed, when given the opportunity, children design play spaces that are considerably different from the standard playgrounds designed by adults. Vandalism is greatly reduced when children and young people have helped to design their own environment. In general, when the users have participated in the design process—whether in community parks, housing, or other projects—they take better care of their facility.

PEOPLE DESIGNING PLACES

What is needed, then, is a design process that allows the shared site (or a single playscape for younger children—see chapter 6) to evolve from community participation, with the specific involvement of the children and young people who are the primary users. This process is the *participatory design process*, which might be better named *people designing places*. Many participatory design plans have been used around the country in recent years to give community members a voice in how their community is to be built, but people designing places is a truly different model. It carries the people involved through the entire planning and design process, from gaining awareness of the built environment to analyzing needs to developing the architectural or landscaping program and designs.

This process requires careful preparation and coordination. However, if all the preparation and activities involved in the process are given adequate attention, a highly successful design, whether for a community park on a school site or a playscape alone, will result.

Preparation

The initial phase of this participatory design process is preparation. The designer must first identify interest groups, create the steering committee, and schedule meetings and design sessions.

It is important to understand the role of the designer in the process, for it is a vital and difficult one. It is perhaps wisest to use a designer from outside the immediate community, although a local landscape architect or a local architecture firm should also be a part of the team. Such a designer can remain neutral throughout the project, providing advice about site and design problems, yet avoiding involvement in local politics and personality clashes. The outside designer is free of vested interests and can thus give credence and importance to each person's or group's ideas. The designer also stimulates participation and encourages people to express their feelings as the plan is shaped. Ideally, the designer should advise the steering committee on the logistics of organization; offer professional advice and expertise concerning landscape solutions in designing a park or playscape; provide information on children's learning and development; act as a mediator of conflicting interests; and be a continuing prod to action, a soother of hurt feelings, and a promoter of good will. The designer should also use the participants' design ideas to organize and present a formal design solution, which the participants must then review and approve before it is presented to the client.

The next step is to identify all the groups with an interest in the community park project. Depending on the nature of the project and its site, concerned groups may include: local government agencies, such as the parks and recreation department, the zoning board, and the planning commission; the school board, superintendent, and principal in charge of the school site; neighborhood groups, such as a block organization or homeowners' committee; local preservation and historical societies; businessmen's organizations; school faculty and staff; parent associations; interested community members not necessarily affiliated with a group; and, above all, the children and youth who will use the park. These people should be invited to form a representative steering committee to guide and oversee the planning process and to make some of the difficult final decisions. They must make summary recommendations concerning the data amassed, and present a final program that meets the needs of all the interest groups as fully as possible. Such a broad-based committee is in an excellent position to be truly responsive to community needs and demands, and to reconcile differing points of view.

The final step is to organize meetings of the steering committee and of the community, including large and small group meetings, design sessions, and follow-up meetings. During these meetings information abut the project is gathered or disseminated, needs are determined, and alternatives are formulated, reviewed, and refined. Open discussion is encouraged to identify the issues and priorities involved and to develop a consensus regarding the structure and scope of the project. Members of each interest group are invited to share their fears and concerns in an informal and friendly atmosphere. The process attempts to bring people together, to increase awareness of the built environment, to help people express their feelings and needs, and to encourage them to discuss ways to solve their problems.

The Process

Interest group participation begins with the first steering committee meeting, during which design sessions and small group meetings are scheduled. The public meetings should begin with a large meeting to which everyone interested in the project is invited. At this meeting the site, scope, and preliminary budget of the project are presented. The steps of the participatory design process should also be explained. Smaller group meetings should then be held, so that members of each representative group may have an opportunity to present their ideas, discuss their interests, and express their fears regarding development of the site. Separate small group meetings are important because they provide a less intimidating atmosphere than a large public meeting. The people who live immediately adjacent to the proposed site are very important to these meetings because they are directly affected by the appearance of, and the activities occurring on, the site. Without their involvement in and acceptance of the project, much will be lost. Since students and children will be the primary users of the park and playscape, their meetings and design sessions are equally important. They will, if the project is successful, use the recreational facilities whenever they can, during school and after-school hours, on weekends, and during vacation time. They should participate in the whole process, in the committee meetings as well as smaller group meetings, and should indicate what they use and like and what new facilities and changes they would like to see on the school site.

In addition, several design sessions should be held. These consist of planning and design exercises that not only allow participants to present their specific design ideas, but also increase their awareness of the built environment, landscape architecture and architecture, space use, activities and activity settings. Follow-up sessions to analyze the results of each planning session are also important.

After the first public meeting, the following sequence—repeated as often as necessary—works best: design session; follow-up session; small group meeting to discuss design session results; and large public meetings and committee meetings to share all the groups' ideas and wishes and to disclose the similarities and differences of each group's solutions.

The Result

Gradually, from this sequence of meetings, a design program emerges that satisfies the needs of all those affected. Many different desires and concerns, some of which school and public officials were probably not aware, are likely to emerge. Thus, rather than a project that angers and incites the community, a project with which everyone is comfortable can evolve.

A CASE STUDY: THE CENTRAL PARK PROJECT, GRAND RAPIDS, MICHIGAN

Grand Rapids has been faced with the same problems that occur in many cities in the United States. Deteriorating downtown neighborhoods, in this case the historical Heritage Hill; school sites perceived as having a negative effect both on the community and on children's learning and development; and increasing declines in school enrollment all plague the city. This was the setting for the Central Park Project.

The ailments of Heritage Hill are endemic to communities of this type across the nation. It is an older neighborhood adjacent to the changing city center and is thus affected by such outside forces as the attraction of the suburbs, the mobility of the two-car family, and absentee landlords. It has an aging population, a deteriorating older housing stock, and an eroding tax base. But Heritage Hill also has both the appearance and community spirit of a neighborhood. The city government, the school system, and the local citizens all exhibit strong concerns for what is happening and what will continue to happen there.

The school site adjacent to three schools in Heritage Hill—Central High School, Fountain Elementary School, and Kent Intermediate Skills Center—had been cleared of houses to provide competitive-sports facilities for the high school. There was criticism from the local residents who feared that a competitive-sports facility, such as a football field with spectator stands and a large parking lot, would have a detrimental effect on the

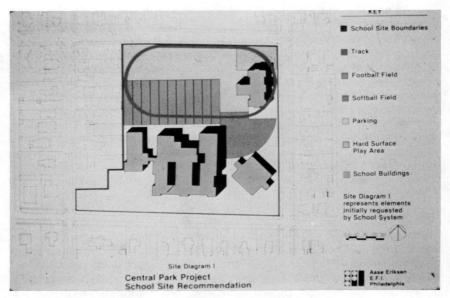

Plan prior to the participatory design process. Central Park Project; Grand Rapids, Michigan.

community. School officials also debated the need for a football field on the site.

The architectural firm of Aase Eriksen Associates of Philadelphia, Pennsylvania, was asked to design the site. With the support of its affiliate, Educational Futures, Inc., a nonprofit educational organization, Aase Eriksen Associates was to study the site for possible ways to fulfill both the school's needs and the neighborhood's demands, and to develop a design solution.

The project began with the establishment of a steering committee that was given the power to advise the school superintendent and board and to represent all interest groups. Included in the Central Park Committee were representatives of the Grand Rapids Public School System, the City Manager's Office, the Grand Rapids Planning Commission, the Grand Rapids Historic Preservation Committee, the Grand Rapids Parks Department, Davenport College, Educational Park, several other community organizations, neighborhood groups, and the principals, faculty, and students from the three schools on the site.

A number of meetings were then held that included the committee, the community, and the Director of Facility Planning, Milton J. Miller, the school system's representative. The results of large and small group meetings, joint and separate design sessions with students, teachers, and community members, and presentations of schematic designs, were considered in the final proposal.

A note should be made here of the valuable role played by Mr. Miller,

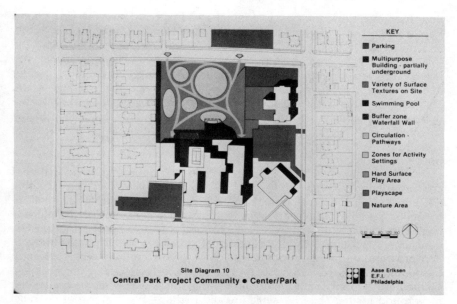

KEY

■ Parking

■ Multipurpose
   Building - partially
   underground

▩ Variety of Surface
   Textures on Site

■ Swimming Pool

■ Buffer zone
   Waterfall Wall

☐ Circulation -
   Pathways

☐ Zones for Activity
   Settings

▨ Hard Surface
   Play Area

■ Playscape

■ Nature Area

Site Diagram 10
Central Park Project Community ● Center/Park

Aase Eriksen
E.F.I.
Philadelphia

Plan proposed by Aase Eriksen as a result of the participatory design process. Central Park Project; Grand Rapids, Michigan.

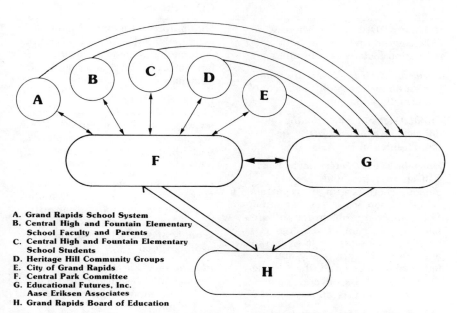

A. Grand Rapids School System
B. Central High and Fountain Elementary
    School Faculty and Parents
C. Central High and Fountain Elementary
    School Students
D. Heritage Hill Community Groups
E. City of Grand Rapids
F. Central Park Committee
G. Educational Futures, Inc.
    Aase Eriksen Associates
H. Grand Rapids Board of Education

Information process. Central Park Project; Grand Rapids, Michigan.

now Associate Superintendent of Fiscal and Physical Planning. The Grand Rapids project was large and complex. In projects that are smaller in scope and may only involve changing a school playground into a playscape, the role played by a person in a position similar to Mr. Miller's is critical. Mr. Miller had the authority to make decisions, the vision and courage to enter into an unknown process and accept new ideas, and the willingness and ability to use his authority to permit new ideas to develop despite the opinions of members of the school system who tended to believe in the seemingly safer status quo. The exciting planning and design results in Grand Rapids could not have been accomplished without Mr. Miller's support and involvement.

In the many meetings held, the various groups expressed different concerns. The overriding concern of the Heritage Hill community was that the impact of new developments on the site would be positive, environmentally, socially, and economically. The main concerns of the Central High School faculty, students, and parents were to improve the existing educational facilities, to add an additional structure for the physical education program, and most important, to strengthen Central High's position in the Grand Rapids School System. The particular concern of the Fountain Elementary School faculty, students, and parents was a larger and better playground for the children, which would perhaps also foster more contact with the high school students.

HERITAGE HILL COMMUNITY CONCERNS

Recreation Deficiency: There is a deficiency of open space and recreation facilities in the area.

Security: Area residents are concerned about the high incidence of crime and vandalism.

Traffic: Heavy traffic volumes and one-way streets impair the residential qualities of Heritage Hill.

Household Characteristics: Over half of the households are one-person. There is a high proportion of retired persons in the community. This can be a problem for the area and its improvement, as often retired persons are on fixed incomes and are unable physically and financially to maintain their homes. There has been an overall population decline in this area.

Old Housing Stock: Most housing is turn-of-the-century. There is evi-

CENTRAL HIGH & FOUNTAIN ELEMENTARY SCHOOL CONCERNS

Multipurpose Building: A multipurpose building for shared school and community activities and other such functions of school and community interest.

Winter Sports Facility: A facility that would meet the requirements for an enclosed space that would provide for winter sports such as basketball, swimming, badminton, and other similar activities.

Landscaping: Implementation of a landscape design to provide both a visual and functional improvement to the site to benefit both the schools and the Heritage Hill neighborhood.

Playground: An attractively and competently designed playground facility for small children for school and community use.

Improve Athletic Facility: General

dence of deterioration of about a third of the area's homes.

Low Ownership Rate: Only eleven percent of the housing units are owner-occupied, which indicates that there is a problem of absentee landlords who may not have a direct concern in the upgrading of the community.

improvement to all existing athletic facilities, especially those physical education facilities for girls.

Educational Facilities: Overall improvement of all educational facilities, especially those at Central High, to ensure the best education for all students.

SPECIFIC SUGGESTIONS

The following suggestions were made for the Central Park site at the first general public meeting:

Tennis	Swimming pool	Evergreens
Natural beauty	Parking	Remove blue windows
Benches for lunch	Gymnasium	Redesign gymnasium
Fountain	High school play area	Underground parking
Track	Open theater	Update girls gym
Lights for evening use	Teenage recreation	locker room
Shell for music/plays	center	Trash cans
Contour	Trees and grass	Lyon street traffic
Updating Fountain	Flowers	Winter ice skating
School	Connect recreational	pond
Underground pool with	activities	All purpose/all
something built on	Fieldhouse open to	weather recreational
top	school and commu-	facility
Drive close to school	nity	Update and renovate
from Lyon Street	Sculpture	entire building

CONSENSUS

The Central School site should become a leisure park providing both the school and the community with outdoor facilities for sports and socializing. If the site is considered as a whole, the community school and community park can be seen as a total community center that can provide both indoor and outdoor activities such as those discussed above. The Fountain Elementary School playground can serve young children not only during school hours, but also for after school play. Planning could eventually include the facilities of the skills center, which could be made available on a broader basis. In this way the community center could encompass the entire site on which these three schools are placed.

Concerns/specific suggestions/consensus.
Central Park Project; Grand Rapids, Michigan.

Concerns

Through the many design sessions and meetings held, the consensus reached was that the school site should be a shared, multiuse space that provides for year-round activities and improves the appearance of the site. To this end, Aase Eriksen Associates proposed a solution for the site as a community center and park, with Central High School offering services to both adolescents and adults. A playscape for Fountain Elementary School children was to form an important portion of the park. Also important were the changes in public attitude—from suspicion to cooperation—and the movement away from traditional design solutions to ones reflective of specific needs. The school site was perceived as a space for meeting social and community needs along with educational ones.

Enthusiasm for the participatory design process and the Central Park Project is apparent in the various comments of Milton J. Miller:

> Participatory planning takes more time. Planners can guide the process, but it can't be forced. Time and a great deal of patience are required because attitudes of people both within the outside the organization have to change.
>
> It is natural to defend what has been done previously in the traditional planning process. Past decisions become planning precedents which eliminate the risk of developing new ideas. The planner feels very secure in proposing plans which have been previously used.
>
> In traditional planning the central office staff is much more involved than the local school staff in giving direction to the project. There is a narrow scope of elements that go into the development. In participatory planning, people from the community, parents of students, and students themselves are included. A much broader picture emerges of how to develop the site so that it is usable for the total community.
>
> When community members have an opportunity to participate in planning, they really come to know and appreciate the process of planning. They become equal partners and are soon saying *we* rather than *they*. They become interpreters of the planning process and promoters of the project when they talk with others in the community.

Program Considerations and Recommendations

The result of the participatory planning process in Grand Rapids was a lengthy list of program considerations and specific design recommendations that addressed these considerations. It was agreed that the site design should:

- serve the needs of students and faculty
- be an amenity to the surrounding community
- invite young and old to visit, linger, and relax
- afford children with opportunities to explore and wonder
- provide children with the experience of well-designed, lively settings
- provide for the needs of all age groups, and for the interaction between age groups
- provide for a variety of sensory experiences through the use of varying textures and materials
- support learning and development
- provide for supervision, so children can be permitted to move freely

The design recommended to meet these considerations was a community park of 2½ acres that included a playscape and was landscaped so that it became a visual as well as a recreational amenity to the surrounding community. It was planned so that various zones, defined as spatial areas,

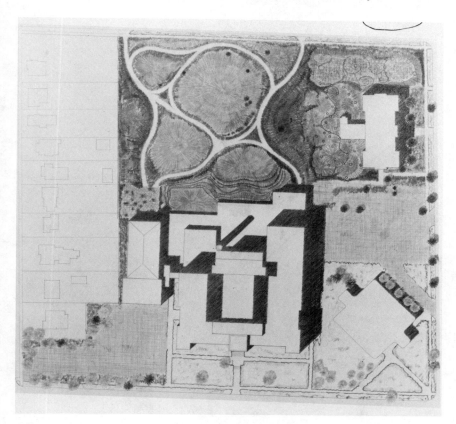

Site plan. Central Park Project; Grand Rapids, Michigan.

would accommodate the many activity needs that were identified by participants in the design process. These zones are general spaces for different
kinds of activities relating to play, learning, socializing, leisure time, or
recreation.

The seven zones that make up Central Park are:

ZONE A: An open field in the northeast corner of the park that provides
space for such activities as ball playing, frisbee tossing, and other group field
games. It is adjacent to Zone F to accommodate a greater distribution of
people and groups during community picnics and other special events.

ZONE B: Located near the main entrance to Central High School, this
zone affords a space for group gatherings and is a natural collecting point.
Stepped seating along an earth embankment accommodates informal gatherings, providing high school students with a place to meet. It can also
service more formal gatherings, such as outdoor lectures, dramatic productions, and school exercises.

ZONE C: Designed as a terrace/patio area, Zone C is located in the
southwest corner of the site and accommodates outdoor eating, chess and
table games, and other social activities around tables and benches.

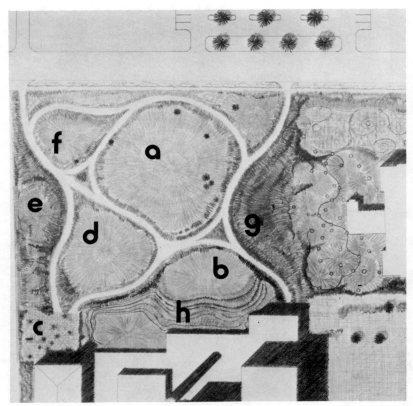

Legend

a	ball play	e	quiet
b	gathering	f	picnic
c	patio	g	nature
d	small gatherings	h	stepped seating

Zones for activities. Central Park Project; Grand Rapids, Michigan.

ZONE D: A place for more quiet, self-contained activities is found here. Zone D is shielded from neighboring Zones A and F with trees and shrubs to provide privacy and screen out noise. It includes a shallow hollow that can be flooded for wintertime ice-skating.

ZONE E: Along the eastern side of the site, Zone E offers a quiet enclave for reading, contemplation, and other such activities. The buffer wall, which serves as a visual and acoustic barrier between the park and Prospect Avenue, provides a pleasant background for the area.

ZONE F: This zone is a picnic area, located to the northeast of Zone A. It is adjacent to Zone A in order to absorb spillover from the playing fields during community gatherings.

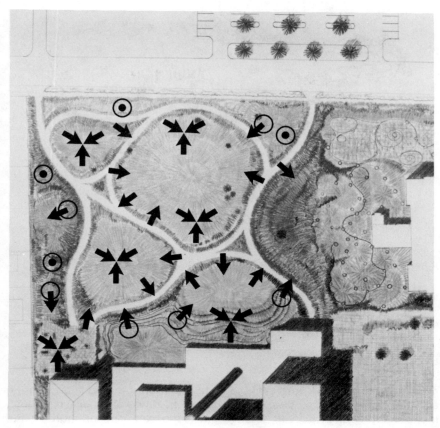

Legend

 interaction with others   ← removed observation

← direct observation   ⊙ privacy

Activity settings: sitting. Central Park Project; Grand Rapids, Michigan.

ZONE G: This zone contains the nature area and playscape intended primarily for the students of Fountain Elementary School.

These zones were created to separate activity settings according to the types of activities they would accommodate (determined during the participatory design process), and the size of the groups that would use them.

It was finally agreed that the park must accommodate the following activities:

- Sitting (resting, reading, contemplating, talking, picnicking)
- Eating
- Walking
- Running
- Ball playing

Sitting setting. Central Park Project; Grand Rapids, Michigan.

- Playacting/theater
- Ice-skating
- Tennis
- Viewing
- Gardening/ecology

Designing a park and playscape to accommodate so many varied activities is a challenging task. In Grand Rapids, it was approached through the development of activity settings that supported one or more of the chosen activities.

Any activity listed above might occur in a variety of settings; for example, people may choose to sit in a large open space in order to sun themselves, or they may choose to sit in a secluded spot in order to read or talk. The designer of the park can suggest certain appropriate activities to be carried on in a particular setting.

The following are samples of the activity settings designed for the park and general recommendations for the development of such settings.

Sitting

Settings that provide for great individual privacy should suggest activities such as reading, and contemplation.

There should only be one seat or bench in this setting. The setting should be removed from other activity settings and from paths. An acoustical and spatial boundary should be highly defined. A provision may be made to signal that such a setting is occupied to avoid disturbance. The view from without should remain closed, while the view from within should be carefully controlled. Focus is of prime importance; a natural feature, (such as a rock or tree or bush) or a man-made feature (such as a column

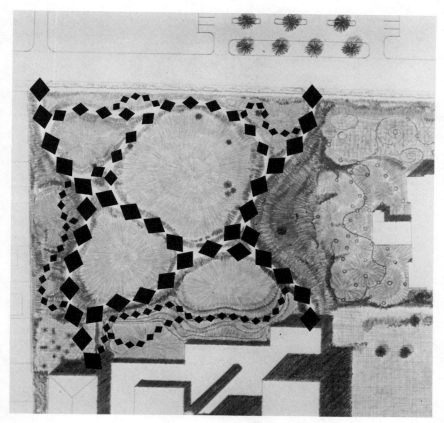

Legend

◆◆ directed   ◆◆◆◆ exploring

◆ ◆ casual (nondirected)

Activity settings: walking. Central Park Project; Grand Rapids, Michigan.

or plaque or ground texture) can be used to provide such a focus. The setting may be recessed to create a pocket of privacy.

Walking

Activity settings that accommodate the individual's need for non-directed activity could include a path for casual strolls to admire various views or plants.

The path shape should have many directions so that views change frequently. The path's edges should provide two types of views: views through the edge into the park and views just beyond the edge to local plantings and artifacts. The edge should therefore be bordered by a sur-round of trees and bushes that vary in thickness and width to help create

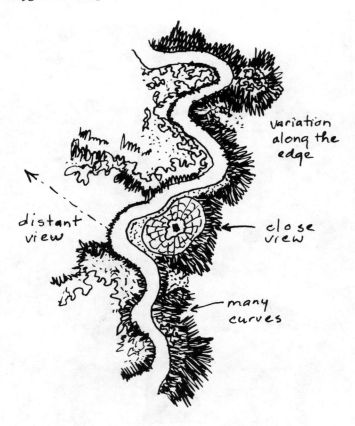

Walking setting. Central Park Project; Grand Rapids, Michigan.

this variety of close and distant views. The surface texture itself may vary in order to emphasize the transitional character of the path.

Viewing

Activity settings that provide for the observation of spaces at a remove or views of a vista should be planned at the edge of open fields.

The observer may be sitting or leaning against an approximately waist-high wall. Ideally the observer's space should be elevated slightly, 12 to 18 inches above the adjacent space, to provide the observer with a broader vista.

The view should be framed, perhaps by trees or shrubs that contain the view. Views should also be planned so that a hierarchy of open areas can be observed. That is, the observer should be able to see adjacent fields and perhaps landmarks outside the park itself. A distant landmark will aid the experience of a view into depth.

The setting should be adjacent to a path for accessibility, but should be designed to face away from the main path.

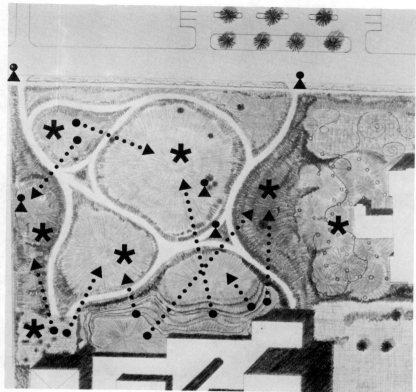

Legend

👤 landmarks   ✳ activity pockets

◀·····● vistas

Activity settings: sitting and viewing. Central Park Project; Grand Rapids, Michigan.

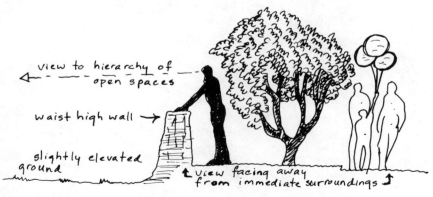

Viewing setting. Central Park Project; Grand Rapids, Michigan.

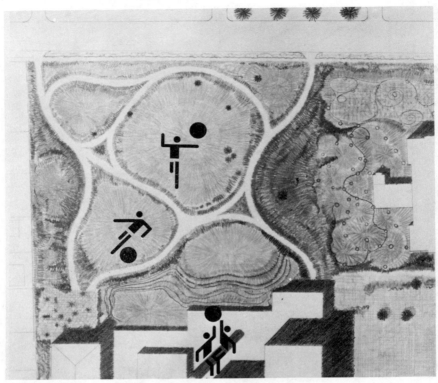

Legend   contained (court games)   uncontained (baseball)

    semi-contained (soccer)

Activity settings: ball play. Central Park Project; Grand Rapids, Michigan.

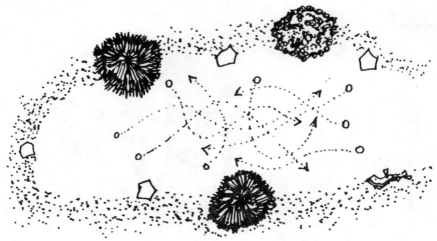

Ball play setting. Central Park Project; Grand Rapids, Michigan.

Fountain Elementary School playscape; Grand Rapids, Michigan.

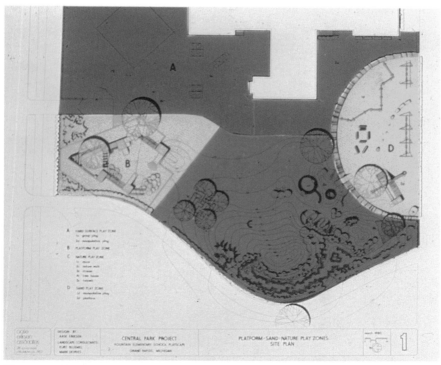

Play zones. Fountain Elementary School playscape; Grand Rapids, Michigan.

Platform structure for younger children. Fountain Elementary School playscape; Grand Rapids, Michigan.

Above and below. *Fantasy playscape drawings from design sessions with Fountain Elementary School children; Grand Rapids, Michigan.*

Facing page, top. *Tire sculpture. Fountain Elementary School playscape; Grand Rapids, Michigan.*

Facing page, center and bottom. *Playscape in use. Fountain Elementary School playscape; Grand Rapids, Michigan.*

Children's playscape design drawing. Fountain Elementary School playscape; Grand Rapids, Michigan.

Children's playscape design drawing. Fountain Elementary School playscape; Grand Rapids, Michigan.

Play equipment designed to reflect children's design-session drawings. Fountain Elementary School playscape; Grand Rapids, Michigan.

Play equipment designed to reflect children's design-session drawings. Fountain Elementary School playscape; Grand Rapids, Michigan.

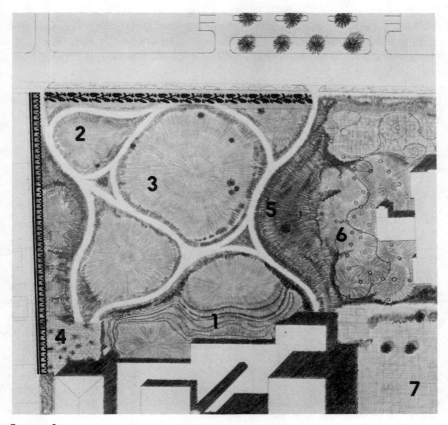

Legend

❧❧❧	planting buffer at Lyon Street	**4**	patio
▥▥▥	waterfall wall buffer	**5**	nature
1	stepped seating	**6**	playscape
2	level for picnic	**7**	parking
3	level for ball play		

Landscaping. Central Park Project; Grand Rapids, Michigan.

Ball Playing

Activity settings for semicontained ball play could be characterized by such games as open-field soccer, touch football, or a pickup game of volleyball. These activities are the most common games played in a park, as they can be accommodated without the burdens of regulation goals and boundaries and can be played on a variety of surfaces.

The goals may be natural landmarks, such as a grove of trees on two sides of a field, or they may be added to the setting, for example, by including a volleyball net or arranging logs and stones for a soccer goal. The ground should not be too hilly and ideally should be surrounded by a slight incline to create an enclave for ball play.

The boundaries will be loosely defined, but scattered plantings within the open field can suggest the bounds of the game. In addition, such visual cues help form a screen between players and spectators.

Chapter 6.
The Playscape

Chapters 3 and 4 detailed the history of two major types of playgrounds. The traditional playground, covered by hard surfaces, contains fixed apparatus and ball-playing areas and is primarily intended for physical exercise that is usually unsupervised. Such playgrounds provide open spaces and easily maintained equipment of familiar design, but they also have serious drawbacks. The desire for simple maintenance has led to the use of dangerous hard surfaces under equipment and a lack of plantings. These playgrounds are uninteresting, and equally important, they do not stimulate the child's emotional, social, and intellectual development. Playgrounds created since the 1950s all too often have not improved upon the traditional playground. They frequently lack important elements such as soft textures, manipulative areas, sand and water, quiet spaces, nature areas, and provisions for dramatic/fantasy play. They allow no experimentation with the physical environment, thus preventing the child from learning to manipulate his surroundings.

The adventure playground, developed as an alternative to the traditional playground, provides many of these missing parts. Its main purpose is to present supervised creative play opportunities, thus avoiding the single-minded purpose of the traditional playground. It is also much more likely to contribute significantly to the learning and development of the child, not only physically but emotionally, socially, and intellectually as well. The adventure playground is an admirable concept; however, it has not been widely accepted in America because of its unsightly appearance and the need for a play leader.

The solution to modern playground design is therefore to create a play environment that combines the best feature of the adventure playground—the stimulation of creative and manipulative play—with the best feature of the traditional playground—play areas that do not require paid supervisors and that are recognized as playgrounds by adults. Such a play environment must provide a variety of activity settings, surfaces, textures, and equipment; it must incorporate sand and water play, nature areas, and manipulative materials; and it must stimulate the child's learning and development in all areas.

Such a playground would be better labeled a *playscape*: a carefully designed and landscaped outdoor environment that supports and suggests activities that are an essential part of the child's learning and development (physical, emotional, social, and intellectual). It affords spatial and textural diversity, recognizing that play is a continuous process that occurs through time and space. It acknowledges the need children feel for a place of their own that is secure against adult intrusion yet accommodates the adult's concern for ease of supervision. It provides for active and quiet areas, informal sitting places for children and adults, and special spaces for manipulative play.

A playscape is a unique concept. It acknowledges the importance of play as a basis for learning and development; it takes into account the effects of the physical environment on play; and, if designed through the participatory design process, it allows children to contribute to the planning and design of their own environment. Each playscape described in the case studies in this chapter is based on these principles.

The playscape seeks to provide activity settings for children of various ages—and therefore in different stages of development—on the same site. Although there must be some separation of areas and equipment, the playscape encourages children of different ages to mingle and play together by the proximity of their separate zones and in the shared zones of nature play, ball play, and so forth.

The playscape is adaptable to any size school site (or day-care center). Thus, if a school site is small or attached to a single elementary school or day-care center, the site can still include the desired zones.

In addition, the participatory design process can be applied to a playscape alone through the series of design sessions and follow-up meetings described below. The children can take part in the actual planning and design of their own playscape and, in so doing, become involved in and learn from the built environment around them. Because of its important effect on their lives and play, children need to learn more about the built environment and the ways in which it acts upon and can be changed by them. Participation in the planning and design of a playscape provides an excellent opportunity for this kind of education.

The playscape is based on several significant characteristics of play. For example, play is a series of linked activities and pauses, movement and rest. The physical design of the playscape takes this into account. For example, the platform play zone provides elevated spaces—for pausing, resting, observing, and inventive games—connected by linking activity areas that encourage movement and exercise. The linkages offered between activity settings are multiple and branching. That is, they offer several choices to the child, and lead to activities of different difficulties that may challenge the child to test himself or allow him to choose safe, familiar activities. Furthermore, the playscape allows manipulation of the environment: sand, water, and movable objects are provided in both the sand play zone and the nature play zone. Finally, the playscape includes nature as an important stimulant to a child's learning and development. Sloped grassy areas for sitting in warm weather and for sledding in winter, water to play in and with, and plant areas where children may touch, smell, taste, even pick a flower, are all part of the playscape.

A playscape is not only an outdoor learning environment for children, but an amenity to the whole community. It is a green attractive space and can be designed to blend with the atmosphere of its surroundings, whether an older residential area with historical houses or an inner-city apartment area. The size of the site on which the playscape is located matters less than the improvement it makes to the neighborhood. The playscape accommodates the children's need for a place of their own, and by providing informal settings for sitting, satisfies adults' concern for supervision as well.

USING THE PARTICIPATORY DESIGN PROCESS

Although members of every interest group in a community are likely to be involved in the planning and design of a community park (as described in chapter 5), the planning and design of a playscape focuses more upon the children. Their needs and desires are paramount, although parents, teachers (if a school site is involved), and recreation leaders (if a municipal site is involved) should also be consulted.

Children can and should be involved in the actual design process. They have an intuitive understanding of play, its forms and purposes. Through the participatory design process, their understanding of their own needs and desires can be combined with the professional knowledge of educators and the technical skills of the designer. The result is a playscape that meets the requirements of all involved. Children provide important contributions to the design process. A playscape that does not take their ideas and desires into account will likely be neglected by them, like so many expensive architectural playgrounds designed for impressiveness rather than for inventive play.

The participatory design process, when applied to a playscape, is likely to be less complicated and shorter than when applied to a community park. The design sessions are at the heart of the process when dealing with children. They involve the participants in hands-on activities that relate to the various steps in the design process. They can consist of one or several sessions, last from two hours to all day, and involve individual or combined interest groups. Design sessions for children can be geared to the participants' level of understanding and skill. The specific sessions described here are for children, since designers are less likely to have worked with these users before.

A sequence of design sessions that takes the participants through the stages of the design process is the best plan. The whole process, from walking tours to the construction of final models for a play environment, is carefully conceived to bring about an awareness of the surrounding built environment and to elicit the children's responses to their own playground space in order to gain a clear sense of their needs, desires, and values.

The initial sessions serve to create an awareness of the built environment in general and of the project site in particular, perhaps through the use of walking tours on the site and into the community. Here, participants learn to see many construction details for the first time; they are, in effect, learning about landscape architecture and architecture. In the intermediate sessions, the participants are divided into smaller groups, each assisted by the designer, and are taught to work with architectural tools and drawings and to discuss possibilities for the project. These sessions analyze activities considered for the site and the available space, and then develop program specifications. In the final design sessions, the participants actually begin to design and to develop program solutions for the site based on the activity and space analyses they have already completed. These sessions involve the creation of drawings and models under the guidance of the designer. As they analyze their own two-dimensional drawings and three-dimensional models, as well as those of other groups, the participants learn even more about landscape architecture and architecture and about the design process.

For each of the design sessions, it is necessary to have additional follow-up sessions during which the participants report, discuss, analyze, and debate the results of the design session. Only through this means can an eventual consensus regarding the use of the site be achieved. If the site is a school site, it is important that the teachers conduct follow-up sessions in the classroom, to allow more time for the children to work on their analyses and plans, to provide greater continuity for the children in the design process, and to make the children's discussions and plans more realistic. If the site is not a school site, follow-up sessions should be conducted with recreation leaders.

The Built Environment Awareness Design Session

The built environment awareness design session, the first session, should introduce the participants to the built environment by examining the site. This is the first step toward informed participation in the design process.

The built environment is architecture in its broadest sense. It is the towns, roads, schools, parks, houses, playgrounds and the spaces that connect them. It frames our actions and in many ways determines the shape of our lives. In a playscape, the built environment means not only the site plan, but also the spatial arrangement of equipment, the pattern of children's and adults' activity settings, the interpersonal distancing the playscape allows, and so forth. In addition, it is the environment *around* the playscape, that is, the neighborhood. The nature and quality of the playscape will be affected by its setting, whether it is in an open area of a park, a space between high-rise buildings, or a place beside a school of traditional design.

The first design session should include a walking tour of the site and its neighborhood. The designer must make the site and surrounding area seem new and unfamiliar by helping the participants to discover architectural details, topographical characteristics, and other environmental elements they have not previously noticed. The participants must learn to *see* what they have looked at a hundred times. This sudden awareness of the built environment will make the site and neighborhood suddenly appear interesting, a place to really investigate and ask questions about.

As an immediate follow-up to the walking tour, the participants should share their discovery through discussions or presentations of activities they engaged in on the tour. Even if the environment is negative—full of run-down housing or vacant lots—the participants will likely have found more good things than they realized were there. They will see and appreciate the possibilities for improvement by realizing the value of what they have. The result will be a more positive attitude toward the possibility for change.

Another follow-up session could involve the analysis of the site and neighborhood in the abstract form of maps, lists of characteristics, and photographs. This session would introduce children to the difficult task of recognizing patterns in space and estimating their effects on patterns of living.

Design session: walking tour of neighborhood. Fountain Elementary School; Grand Rapids, Michigan.

The Fantasy Playscape Design Session

The fantasy playscape design session seeks to encourage freedom and innovation in design. The children are asked to design a fantasy playscape. There are no limits placed on the size, site, or elements to be contained within the playscape; it could be located anywhere, contain anything. It is to be simply an environment for play, not necessarily related to anything the children have seen before.

The main objective of this session is to unlock the children's imaginations. Participants usually have difficulty trying to translate needs and desires into spatial configurations. Even experienced designers often tend to respond with conventionalized spaces to a particular design need. The fantasy playscape exercise helps remove preconceived notions of what a playground should be and allows children to reinvent spaces and concepts for play. An extended period of time is needed for children to explore and develop their imaginary play environments and to create a number of drawings to their own satisfaction.

The range of suggestions will be very great—from a gravity-free playscape in outer space to a crisscrossed roadway for bicycles, roller skates, and skateboards—but some patterns of preference will likely emerge.

The Activity Analysis Design Session

The activity analysis design session is another preparatory exercise in built environment awareness. Prior to involving the children in the actual

Fantasy playscape design session. Fountain Elementary School; Grand Rapids, Michigan.

design process, they should learn how to use such basic architectural tools as site plans and measuring devices and to understand the difference between an activity and an activity setting. In this session, the children are given a site plan—perhaps a blueprint of the old playground—and asked to map their activities on it. They then go to the site and compare the plan with the actual physical space. They then compile a list of the play activities they currently engage in; a list of these activities in order of preference; and, finally, a list of activities they would like to have that are not currently accommodated by the playground.

One of the purposes of this session is to acquaint the children with the difference between activities and activity settings. The relationship between activities and their settings is usually so closely intertwined that it is common to describe an activity in terms of the place in which it is performed without fully comprehending the relationship. A common example of this confusion is the description of a seesaw (a physical setting) instead of balancing (an activity). This is a problem not only for children, but also for adults, both nondesigners and designers. By clearly defining activities and separating them from the conventional spaces or structures that support them, it is possible to reestablish the relationship between activity and setting, and perhaps design new settings for familiar activities.

The task of defining activities, recognizing the difference between activities and settings, and locating them on a site plan is quite difficult. But with the established list of desired activities prepared in the previous design session, the children can be encouraged in follow-up sessions to suggest

Activity analysis design session: studying the site. Fountain Elementary School; Grand Rapids, Michigan.

how some of their activities and desires can be accommodated on their playscape. No designs are to be suggested at this time, but the children are, in effect, developing their own program for such a design.

The Playscape Design Session

The playscape design session involves the children in making real design suggestions in the form of schematic designs for both the spaces and the equipment of their playscape. First, it is important to review their acquired knowledge of the relationship between the actual measurements of the site and the scaled blueprints of the area. The children are then asked to plan spaces where various activities can take place. That is, using a site plan, the children draw a map on which they select different areas for different activities, using bubbles to indicate these spaces. To do this, the children must consider the available space in relation to the long lists of activities—both desired and preferred—that they have already established.

The children are then asked to draw actual play settings and equipment that will accommodate the list of activities they have created. They are then asked to explain their drawings in order to illustrate the spaces and equipment they would create.

The relationship between the children's drawings and the suggested list of activities may not always be clear. Often the drawings will suggest relationships among activities that were not evident in previous mappings. Activities already on the lists are not always accommodated by the equipment drawn. Some drawings may still rely on the fantasy elements of the fantasy playscape design session; other drawings may be dominated by conventional playground equipment. However, from these drawings, general patterns and relationships will emerge quite clearly. The lists, plans, and conventional and fantastic drawings will reveal the children's desires for a playscape design.

Design sessions held for the creation of playscapes suggest such settings and equipment as:

- elevated spaces, often in the form of treehouses, and equipped for various activities including climbing, sliding, observing, and swinging
- active and quiet spaces
- private (as opposed to group) spaces
- natural areas with sand, water, and plants, for molding, building, and cultivating
- curvilinear slides with intricate climbing approaches
- hard-surface game areas, with colored lines defining boundaries and goals
- tunnels
- a great variety of swinging, gliding, and balancing equipment

Children are likely to arrange a number of pieces of equipment in relation to one another and in relation to their overall concept of play. This *linkage* is an important characteristic of children's designs, and their drawings reveal their perceptions of *how* to link activities to one another. While their drawings will vary, two general patterns of linkage are likely to emerge. One is a branching pattern, where a choice of routes based on develop-

Playscape design session: linkages and circular patterns. Fountain Elementary School; Grand Rapids, Michigan.

Playscape model design session. Fountain Elementary School; Grand Rapids, Michigan.

mental stages of differing difficulties lead from one activity to another. The other is a circular pattern, accommodating movement and rest, that leads from one setting to another.

The Playscape Model Design Session

This session is directed at having the children conceive their playscape designs in three-dimensional form. The children should be presented with scaled plans of the site to serve as the basis of their models. The models could be made with clay of various colors, as it is easy to work with and children are familiar with it. The models should be worked on in groups, thus encouraging the children to share perceptions and suggestions concerning the order and configuration of the playscape.

The models should not just be direct three-dimensional representations of the two-dimensional drawings done earlier. Instead, the children are encouraged to rethink and add to their designs. However, the drawings do serve as the basis for their work. Before the children begin, they should once again review the environmental knowledge they have acquired concerning activities, needs, and types and patterns of activity settings.

The purpose of this design session is to encourage the children to draw conclusions about the relationships among desired activities, possible linkages, and the settings where they could be accommodated, by manipulating these relationships in three-dimensional form. The design sessions have progressively decreased in their level of abstraction, from fantasy drawing, to listing desired activities, to drawing desired play settings, to building three-dimensional models. The final result is that the children have developed an architectural program that fulfills their needs, and in so doing they have addressed the reality of the built environment.

Follow-up sessions for this session should allow the children to continue work on their playscape models and to develop further models of equipment. An art teacher may introduce the children to other materials for modeling as well.

The Design Session with Concerned Adults

The perceptions and goals of the adults involved—parents, teachers, and recreation leaders—are very important to the playscape's success. Thus a design session for adults is a valuable part of the design process for a playscape.

To begin this session, the participants should list play activities with which they are familiar and define some of the characteristics of these play activities as they relate to the level and duration of activity, and any safety problems they attribute to the activity. Specific problems with the site (for example, if the current site is already a playground) should be discussed. These may include ease of observation, activity conflict, circulation, and environmental and weather conditions.

The list of activities and characteristics should then be carefully analyzed by the participants. First, however, the concept of the playscape should be reviewed: that play has physical, emotional, social, and intellectual objectives and therefore is a fundamental part of the learning process; that the participation of all the potential users of the playscape in the actual design is necessary for its success. While the children are the primary users, the adults will act as the administrators and managers of the playscape. It is therefore imperative that observations and concerns of both children and adults are addressed in the early stages of design.

After this review of the playscape concept, the participants should be asked to develop matrix charts of the play activities and games that they have listed. The activities and games should be described as either active or passive. The number of children involved, the approximate duration of the activity, and whether the form of play presents safety concerns should also be considered.

The information gathered from this session with adults balances the information gained from the sessions with children. The adults involved become committed to understanding children's play needs and to recognizing the potential of the playscape concept for satisfying those needs. Follow-up sessions should involve both children and adults. The result will be a heightened awareness of the children's needs and desires.

A CASE STUDY: THE FOUNTAIN ELEMENTARY SCHOOL PLAYSCAPE, GRAND RAPIDS, MICHIGAN

The entire series of six design sessions and follow-up sessions was held to prepare for the design of the playscape for elementary school children,

Walking tour: looking for building details. Fountain Elementary School; Grand Rapids, Michigan.

which was part of the larger Central Park Project in Grand Rapids, Michigan. In many cases, the follow-up sessions were additional class periods used to allow the children to complete the drawings or models begun during the design sessions.

The following is a sample of the many charts, drawings, and models made by the children during the participatory design process. As each child produced several pieces of material during each design session, it is not possible to reproduce more than a small portion of the results of their work. The material presented here has been selected to illustrate both the process and some of the more important contributions made by the children to the final design of their playscape.

During the walking tour, conducted as part of the built environment awareness design session, the children were given lists of architectural and building details to look for in the neighborhood. These lists helped them to discover parts of buildings they had not seen before and to begin to learn about architecture and the importance of details.

The second design session resulted in many fascinating designs for a fantasy playscape. The drawings reproduced here illustrate the circular slides, connected structures, and treehouse that were eventually incorporated into the playscape.

During the activity analysis design session, children were asked to create a list of activities that they could, or would in the future, perform on a playground. Then, with the guidance of the design consultant, they were asked to analyze their lists to determine the various settings each activity

Activity/game matrix charts. From the children's design session, Fountain Elementary School, Grand Rapids, Michigan.

ACTIVITIES	Active/ Passive	Quiet/ Noisy	Approx. Group Size	Environmental Needs	Location & Orientation	Equipment	Time Span	A = grade 1–3 B = grade 4–6	Special Concerns
Climbing	active	noisy	small	grass		jungle gym	15 min	A & B	soft place to land
Sliding	active	noisy	small	grass		tunnel slide	15 min	A	safety
Playing & Building in Sandbox	passive	quiet	large	sand		sandbox	15 min	A	
Jumping	active	noisy	one at a time, small group	grass		spring-board	15 min	B	
Pretending (Fantasy Play)	active and/or passive	noisy and/or quiet	small to large	grass		wooden fort	15–30 min	A & B	

Activity	Type	Noise	Group Size	Surface	Location	Equipment	Time	A & B	Safety
Sitting	passive	quiet	small or large	grass		benches, trees	5 min	A & B	
Playing with Toy Cars	active to passive	quiet	small	blacktop		toy cars	15 min	A	
Jumping Rope	active	noisy	1–3	blacktop		rope	15 min	A	
Tag	active	quiet	small	obstacles to move in & out of soft surface	north side		15–30 min	A & B	safety
Reading	passive	quiet	small	benches, stumps, stools, enclosures	near bldg		15 min	A & B	
Swinging	active	quiet	small	soft surface	near bldg	swings	15–30 min	A & B	
Ice Skating	active	noisy	varies	hard surface (ice)	rink	watering equipment for ice	15-30 min	B	safety

ACTIVITIES	Active/ Passive	Quiet/ Noisy	Approx. Group Size	Environmental Needs	Location & Orientation	Equipment	Time Span	A = grade 1–3 B = grade	Special Concerns
Sliding or Sledding	active	quiet	varies	snow, hills or slopes		sleds	15–20 min	A & B	safety
Running/Jogging	active	quiet	small	soft surface	completely around school		varies	A & B	how big an area to be covered
Punching Bags	active	quiet	1	covered area, firm ground	close to building	punching bags	5 min	B	
Climbing & Sliding	active	quiet and/or noisy	varies	soft sur- face below	sunny area	ropes, poles, platform	varies	A & B	
Snow Ball Target Throwing	active	noisy/quiet	varies	snow		target	varies	A & B	
Bouncing	active	noisy	1–2	soft surface	anywhere	trampo- line/re- silient soft surface	5–30 min	grades K-6	

Activity								
Climbing	active	quiet or noisy	varies	hill with varied surface	hill		varies	A & B
Climbing (Objects)	active	quiet	small or large	varied soft materials, soft surface	anywhere	rubber tires, etc.	varies	A & B
Roller Skating	active	quiet	small	hard		skates, safety pads, skate rest bar	20–30 min	B

GAMES	Active/ Passive	Quiet/ Noisy	Approx. Group Size	Environ- mental Needs	Location & Orientation	Equipment	Time Span	A = grade 1–3 B = grade 4–6	Special Concerns
Basketball	active	noisy	large	pavement	courts	basketball, baskets, backboards	15 min	A & B	
Softball	active	noisy	large (15)	pavement	field	baseball diamond, balls, bats,	30 min	B	
Kick Ball	active	noisy	large (15)	pavement	court	ball	15 min	grades 3–6	
Tennis	active	quiet	4	hard (clay) surface	anywhere	court, nets, etc.	10–30 min (or 1 hr)	B or (A & B)	
Tag	active	noisy	large or small	varied surface	spread out	places to hide	varies	A & B	
Hide & Seek	active	quiet	large or small	places to hide	spread out	places to hide	varies	A & B	

	Type	Noise	Size	Surface	Location	Equipment	Time	Group	Notes
Tether Ball	active	noisy	small	blacktop	court	tether ball pole	15 min	B	
Jacks	active	quiet	small or large	blacktop		jacks, ball	5 min	grades 1–4	
Frisbee	active	quiet	4 or 5	hard surface	varies	frisbee	10–15 min	A & B	
Bombardo	active	noisy	10	varies	western part of playground	ball (near wall of school)	15–20 min	B	safety
Touch Football	active	noisy	large (12–16)	soft sun	away from school	football goals	15–30 min	A & B	
Volleyball	active	noisy	large	soft surface (sunny)	away from school	net & volleyball	15–30 min	B	
Soccer	active	noisy	large	soft surface (sunny)	away from school	soccer ball	15–30 min	B	

GAMES	Active/ Passive	Quiet/ Noisy	Approx. Group Size	Environ-mental Needs	Location & Orientation	Equipment	Time Span	A = grade 1–3 B = grade 4–6	Special Concerns
Running Track	active	noisy	small to large	resilient surface	away from building		varies	A & B	
Lines for Relay Type Activities	active	noisy	relays of 4 or more	resilient surface	away from building	sacks; batons	varies	A & B	
4-Square	active	noisy	4	soft dirt	4-square area	ball, 4-square lines	10–25 min	A & B	
Painted Pave-ment Games	active	noisy	varies	hard/soft surface	north of school building	depends on game	varies	A & B	

Hopscotch	active	noisy	2	hand painted on surface	north of school building	stones, flat objects	15 min	A & B
Marbles	active	quiet or noisy	small	soft	away from building	sand	15–30 min	A & B

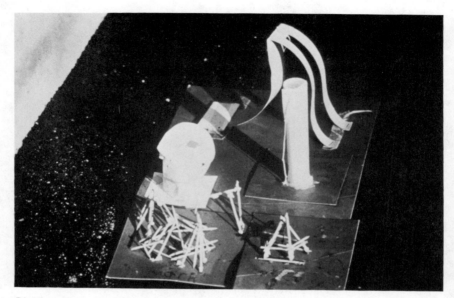

Children's equipment model. Fountain Elementary School; Grand Rapids, Michigan.

would require. The matrix chart is a final summation of the charts produced by the children. The care and attention given to their answers was apparent and led to the creation of many possibilities.

The playscape design session used both bubble diagrams to place activities into groups on the site, and the children's drawings of settings and equipment that would support the activities they had listed in the previous session. The drawings may be studied for the linkages of play activities that the children found important.

The playscape model design session allowed the children to translate their two-dimensional drawings into three-dimensional models of clay.

Finally, the design session with concerned adults—in this case the teachers of Fountain Elementary School—illustrated the differences between the adults' and the children's conceptions of play activities and play equipment.

Translation of Theory into Design Practice

At this point, two major steps in the design of the Fountain School Playscape were completed. First, the designer had attained a thorough knowledge of the developmental needs of children. Second, the children and community members added their input through the participatory design process.

The task now facing the design consultant was to translate the theories of play and development and the information gained from the participatory design process into a design for a playscape. The exact methods by which

Children's model of playscape. Fountain Elementary School; Grand Rapids, Michigan.

ideas and theories can be embodied in actual design choices are difficult to describe, but an extensive analysis of both play theory and the children's ideas was clearly necessary before choices could be made. The charts and outlines that follow represent only the framework of the translation process.

Developmental Needs

The first step was to extract and summarize from the extensive research into child learning and development those concepts relevant to play and playground design. The child's need for stimulation was considered in detail, and while no listing could contain all the specific developmental needs of all children, the following lists include those thought to be of paramount importance. Each item requires separate and thoughtful consideration to determine play activities that will stimulate such learning and development.

PHYSICAL. Physical play involves both gross-motor, large muscle development, and fine-motor or perceptual-motor development. Physical play activities include structured games, such as kickball, four square and hop scotch; nonstructured play, such as climbing, swinging, and sliding; and perceptual and fine-motor activities, such as working on handicrafts, and building a tree fort. The playscape should provide opportunities for physical development that:

- strengthen physical skills by using large and small muscle groups
- develop motor, rhythmic, and kinesthetic sense
- develop dexterity and skill in manipulating objects

- develop hand, eye, and foot coordination
- develop awareness of physical capabilities and limits
- develop body and spatial awareness

EMOTIONAL. Emotional play involves the development of abilities for both independent and cooperative activities. It includes solitary play, group play, participation in structured games, the investigation of rules for non-structured play, cooperating and aiding others, accepting cooperation and aid from others, and a host of self-identifying and group-identifying activities. The playscape should therefore provide opportunities for emotional development that help the child to:

- develop a feeling that he or she will be liked and trusted
- learn to play independently, as well as to accept aid from peers or advice from adults
- develop a growing ability to interact both intellectually and socially with peers for mutual benefit
- learn to play effectively with other children and to value his or her own rights as well as the rights of others
- develop self-identity through feelings of competence, accomplishment, and creativity
- develop a sense of compassion, empathy, and caring for others and their feelings

SOCIAL. Social play involves the development of cooperative modes of play and other forms of social interaction, including games, group projects, observation, or simply conversation. In addition, dramatic and role-playing activities are part of the social aspects of play. The playscape should therefore provide opportunities for social development that help the child to:

- develop an understanding of what is expected of him or her in group situations and why
- increase his or her ability to identify and empathize with others' feelings
- develop a willingness to be part of a group or team
- develop a growing sense of responsibility for group behavior and care of materials
- develop trust and respect for peers and adults
- develop the ability to interact with older children and help younger children
- gain a sense of enthusiasm for group efforts and develop a sense of group goals

COGNITIVE. Cognitive play involves the manipulating, role-playing, problem-solving, constructing, and fantasizing abilities of the child. Providing opportunities for cognitive development will help the child to:

- develop creative thinking; to use intuition and imagination as well as logic
- develop and employ problem-solving skills and strategies with respect to intellectual and social problems

- deal with symbols and various modes of expression, realize their meanings, and use them appropriately
- grow in ability to do, to make, and to create
- express inner creative impulses through dance, song, painting, handicrafts, acting, and the like

Activities

Again, it is not possible to list all of the play activities that children could engage in that would stimulate their learning and development. The following lists are therefore compilations of the activities that should be considered. No playscape could possibly support all play activities, but the aim is to create a playground that will provide settings that suggest as many activities and encourage as much learning and development as possible.

Activities that promote physical growth are:

Sliding	Ordering
Swinging	Manipulating
Rocking	Molding
Climbing	Feeling/handling
Balancing	Sitting/passive activity
Crawling	Observing
Jumping	Digging
Rolling/tumbling	Planting
Pushing/pulling	Exploring/seeking
Hopping/skipping	Water play
Running	Sand play
Throwing/catching	Ball play
Cooperative games	Toy play
Competitive games	Doll play
Building/constructing	Drilling
Walking	Local games
Collecting	
Distributing	
Arranging	
Hiding	

Activities that contribute to emotional growth are:

Homemaking	Handling objects
Creative self-expression	Role-playing
Solitary play	Rebuilding/reconstruction
Personal care	Fantasy play
Risk taking	Ordering

| Music making | Experimenting |
| Group participation | Responding to personal needs |

Activities that promote social growth are:

Cooperative games	Singing/creative noise making
Cooperative problem solving	Obeying rules
Listening	Fact learning
Dancing	Displaying/explaining
Group exploring	Questioning/investigating
Verbal intercourse	Ordering/arranging
Sharing	Group fantasy play
Copying	Experimenting with games
Cooperative projects	Interpersonal care/caring
Planning	Experimenting with objects

Activities that promote cognitive development are:

Listening	Creative self-expression
Problem solving	Rhythmic movement
Observing (intergroup)	Rhythmic noise making
Observing (natural processes)	Imaging/symbolizing
Using tools	Imagining
Making things	Solitary play
Matching, naming, identifying	Mimicking
Spatial orientation	Reading
Drawing	Manipulating
Exploring	Describing
Experimenting (socially)	Writing
Experimenting (nature/materials)	

In reviewing these lists, it is important to give separate and thoughtful considerations to each item. Frequently an activity will stimulate more than one kind of development. Even an activity such as running, which is usually thought of as purely physical, can stimulate emotional, social, and cognitive growth. This development depends upon whether the activity is performed alone, with other children, or in competition; whether the setting is flat and easy to use, or changes directions and is more difficult to use; whether the activity is part of a game conforming to rules or a result of free expression; and so forth. The design of the playscape should support an activity in all of its various forms at different times and places.

Often a single activity listed here might be prompted by several different kinds of settings. For example, the physical activity of climbing must occur in a vertical setting (although the degree of verticality need not always be 90 degrees from the horizontal). At times hand- and toe-holds are required; at other times they are not. Children may climb a hill, a tree, or a pole, and each of these climbs requires different kinds of hand- or toe-holds. It is therefore important to include a variety of climbing devices and settings in a playscape in order for children to learn the physical aspects of climbing.

For the most part, an activity setting should and will encourage more than one activity. For example, the inclusion of a treehouse in a playscape could provide multiple activity settings for multiple activities and stimulate the child's development in more than one area. The climbing structure, the platform, the "house," and the dismounting structure of a treehouse could provide support for such physical activities as climbing, pulling, and swinging; such emotional activities as self-asserting or listening; such social activities as playing house or imagining (fantasy play); and such cognitive activities as problem solving (deciding how to climb) or observing natural processes (the changing leaves of the trees).

Activity Settings

An activity does not occur in empty space but in a real, physical environment. That environment or setting may be appropriate and suggestive of the activity—for example, a study carrel in a library provides a quiet and private atmosphere for reading and study. Or the setting may be inappropriate and hinder the activity—for example, a high school student is not as likely to study in front of the television set as in a library.

As we have noted previously, an activity setting is an activity seen in three dimensions. Any particular activity can occur in many different settings. The designer can only select and put together a limited number of

Children's playscape design. Fountain Elementary School; Grand Rapids, Michigan.

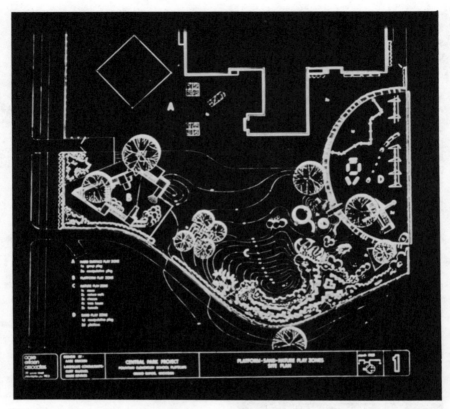

Playscape design by Aase Eriksen. Fountain Elementary School; Grand Rapids, Michigan.

activity settings into a space called a playscape. He or she must therefore choose a combination of settings that will suggest and support as wide a variety of activities as possible, in view of such limitations as site and budget. The wider the variety of activities the play area supports, the richer and more stimulating an environment it will be and the greater the contribution it will make to children's learning and development.

Play Zones

In the Fountain School Playscape, the activity settings that were suggested and designed by the children and adults during the participatory design process were combined with knowledge of children's learning and development. This information was then translated into a design that grouped various activity settings into play zones.

These play zones bring together activity settings according to the children's developmental stages and the types of activities they suggest. The four zones are the *hard-surface play zone,* the *nature play zone,* the *sand play zone,* and the *platform play zone.*

Hard-surface play zone. The hard-surface play zone provides settings for play activities that require an open, hard-surfaced area. The play activities supported by this zone include ball play and running games, as well as such less noisy pursuits as hopscotch, jumping rope, and marbles. These activities usually occur in small or large groups, which may be divided into teams or less formally organized groups. Some special equipment may be required for this kind of play, such as basketball hoops or hopscotch patterns, but the primary requirement is the open, hard-surfaced area.

At Fountain Elementary School, the hard-surface play zone extends along the entire north and west sides of the school building. The area on the north side is separated from the street by a 10-foot-high wooden and wire fence of the same type as the lower fence that surrounds the rest of the playscape. This part of the zone provides a basketball hoop at the east end, as well as boundaries, goal lines, and patterns for various popular games painted on the asphalt. These games include hopscotch and a local favorite known as bombardo. These boundaries and patterns are painted in bright colors to provide visual relief from the expanse of asphalt paving.

On the west side of the school, the paved area is interrupted by an extending wing of the building. This layout provided two somewhat sheltered hard-surface areas conducive to forms of play that do not require a large open space, such as hopscotch or jumping rope. The space on the south side of the extending wall was well suited for smaller children involved in manipulative play, as with trucks or other toys. Its proximity to the manipulative sand area allows smaller children to move back and forth as desired from surface to surface. Because smaller children would use this area, seating for teachers and parents was provided in the form of four benches along one of the walls.

The hard-surface play zone at Fountain Elementary School uses part of a previously existing hard-surface playground, but the rest of the playscape was newly designed and constructed. When the children tire of activities such as ball or running games, they may choose to visit other play zones to pursue other kinds of activities.

Nature play zone. The nature play zone is perhaps the most unusual zone in the playscape. Very few playgrounds on school sites provide green grass, trees, shrubs, and water as part of the environment. But these elements contribute significantly to children's learning and development. The students of Fountain Elementary School asked for such an area, and the nature play zone was designed to support the most important play activities that can occur in such a setting.

At the center of this zone is a 14-foot-high grass-covered mound. It is the highest point of the playscape and supports activities such as sitting, viewing, and, in the winter, sledding. Several activity settings that make use of other natural elements are located at the base of some of the slopes of this mound.

To the southeast, a tunnel and mound area, consisting of three tunnels under small earth mounds, supports activities such as crawling, hiding, climbing, and sliding. The tunnels are made of concrete, but the ends of

Nature zone tunnel and mound area. Fountain Elementary School; Grand Rapids, Michigan.

each duct are covered with rubber gaskets for the children's added safety. Circular openings with sloped walls of large sea-washed rocks, a long slide leading into the sand play zone, and a set of stairs leading down to the grass are also included in this area.

Thus, a child may crawl through a tunnel into an opening and then choose to climb up the sloping sea rock wall, or stairs; continue through the next tunnel into the second opening, and exit up the wall; or continue into the third tunnel and crawl or use the stairs to the top of the mound in order to exit by means of the slide, or stairs. The various activities and options that this area provides for the children is in keeping with the nature of play, that is, the continuous pattern of activities.

To the south of the central mound is a treehouse, which consists of a two-level wooden platform surrounding, but not supported by, a large tree. One side of the treehouse faces the sloping central mound, which permits the slope to serve as natural amphitheater seating with the tree platform as a stage. The platform may be reached by the slope of the mound or by a ladder and is surrounded by a wooden railing. The treehouse is an appropriate setting for a variety of activities such as following, sharing, fantasy play, and "theatrical productions."

Near the treehouse is a water play setting, consisting of a shallow stream of water bordered by the same sea-washed rocks used in the tunnel and mound area. The small, continuous flow of water descends in a winding course and is the setting for water play activities such as sailing small boats, as well as a setting for quiet talk and contemplation.

Children in tunnel. Fountain Elementary School; Grand Rapids, Michigan.

On the north side of the central mound is a maze. It is constructed of numerous poles that support vinyl-covered canvas walls of bright colors such as yellow, orange, red, and white. The maze has been designed so the children can change the panels and thereby change the circulating paths of the maze when they have become very familiar with one pattern. The opportunity to redesign the maze's overall pattern is important in that it allows children who will use the playscape in the future to play a part in designing and maintaining the playscape. The maze supports such play activities as hiding, running, and walking and contributes to the children's intellectual growth in presenting a problem to solve—that is, to discover the pattern of the maze in order to hide or play other games more effectively.

The final area of the nature play area is the nature walk, at the bottom of the western slope of the central mound. It is a quiet area, conducive to conversation, reading, and other restful activities. The walk is lined with raised planters in which the children may plant and cultivate various annual weeds, flowers (including local wildflowers), or shrubs as part of their nature study. The children can smell, touch, look at, and, if weeds and local wildflowers are used, they may even pick the plants without being punished as they might be in a public or private park. A game table with a built-in checkerboard pattern is also provided in this area.

The nature play zone thus combines in all of its areas a large variety of activity settings for such diverse activities as sledding, crawling, water games, hiding, theatrical play, planting and growing, quiet talk, and many others. That so many activities can be suggested by a nature zone indicates the importance of including such an area in any playscape.

Sand play zone. The south side of the sand play zone provides

Nature walk being planted. Fountain Elementary School; Grand Rapids, Michigan.

activity settings for younger children (from preschool through the third grade), although older children may wish to play in this area as well. The entire zone is sand covered, with wood chips also included in all but the manipulative play area, which is covered with sand alone. This zone has a number of areas designed for different activities.

One such area consists of a structure of two connected platforms with various linkages to the ground. These platforms resemble the structures in the platform play zone for older children but are of a difficulty and scale more appropriate to younger children. Platform A has four linkages or connectors leading to and from its deck: there are steps for climbing; bars for climbing; a wide slide on which two or three children may slide down simultaneously; and a suspension bridge to platform B that supports walking, running, and jumping activities. Platform B has three linkages: the suspension bridge to or from platform A; a spiral slide from its deck to the ground; and a ladder for climbing up or down. Platform B also has an enclosed sitting space under the deck with cutout shapes for entering, exiting, or viewing. The platform area also provides ropes for climbing, a metal pole with a bell to ring when the child successfully shimmies to the top, and two large rubber tire swings for group swinging. Also part of the sand play zone are two sets of swings with soft seats for solitary or coordinated swinging.

A third area is the manipulative play area for very young children. This large, open sand pit is defined by a wall of balancing beams and the arc of the boardwalk that surrounds the entire zone. It can be used for sand play inasmuch as the boardwalk has open spaces between boards allowing the sand to fall through and back into the sand play area. The cantilever

Wide slide. Fountain Elementary School; Grand Rapids, Michigan.

construction of the boardwalk, with the main support toward the outside of the boardwalk's arc, also helps to retain the sand. The sand play area is important in providing support for a variety of manipulative activities.

The linked play area, defined by a "wall" of balancing beams, provides a tire sculpture and several jumping poles, as well as the beams themselves, to accommodate various balancing activities. This equipment supports activities such as leapfrogging, jumping, and stepping from one support to another.

The boardwalk that separates the entire zone from the nearby nature play zone provides a setting for running, walking, and sitting, inasmuch as the walk consists of various levels of steps up and down. The boardwalk and balancing areas are placed so as to be linked with the activities that occur in the tunnel and mound area already described. Play can move through tunnels, down the slide, along or over balancing equipment, over the boardwalk, and back into the tunnels without interruption.

Platform play zone. The platform play zone for older children is a series of seven platforms and a mound of spools on a sand base that are connected by multiple and branching linkages. There are three to five connectors or links to or from each platform. The zone is designed so that children of different developmental levels are able to play individually, to share spaces, or to interact in cooperative play.

Play is a series of pauses and movements and the platform/linkage system allows for this natural rhythm. The platforms provide areas for pausing and resting, for viewing the surroundings, and for decision-making concerning the selection of a linkage. Beneath the decks of three platforms are semienclosed areas to provide hiding, private, and resting places. Dexterity is required to crawl into and out of these spaces. The linkages provide several choices of activity. The child can choose to go directly to the next platform or to leave the platform; branching linkages are included from platform D to platforms E and F. The linkages relate to different levels of development, thus encouraging the child to challenge his abilities while allowing him to avoid the challenges he is not yet ready to face.

The platform play zone is designed to encourage the child's physical (including motor and sensory), social, emotional, and cognitive development. Gross and fine motor abilities, including agility, balance, endurance, flexibility, coordination, power, speed, and strength are developed, as are sensory abilities such as spatial awareness, directionality, visual awareness, and tactile awareness. Social, emotional, and cognitive processes and abilities that can be developed include discovery, exploration, decision-making, communication, interaction, sharing, leadership, compromise, and conflict resolution.

The entire platform play zone allows the child to master graded challenges, to develop muscle coordination and sensory awareness, to enjoy an element of risk with alternatives to avoid risk, and to develop social, emotional, and cognitive abilities.

The following lists indicate some options for activities on or from each platform.

Platform A

- Climbing (rope tied like a cargo net)
- Walking, running, jumping (suspension bridge)
- Riding/hanging (pulley)
- Climbing (ladder)
- Walking, running, jumping (suspension bridge)

Platform B

- Sliding, climbing (metal pole)
- Sliding, climbing (rope)
- Climbing (ladder)
- Viewing (tower landing)
- Crawling (steel tube)

Platform C

- Sliding (steel slide)
- Hanging, moving (horizontal metal bars)
- Walking, hopping (stepping logs)

Platform D

- Balancing (two balancing beams—one 3 by 6 inches, one 6 by 6 inches)
- Balancing (tire bridge)
- Crawling (tire bridge)

Platform E

- Climbing (ladder)

- Viewing (landing)
- Climbing, hanging (rope net)

Platform F

- Jumping, stepping (pile of tires)
- Walking, running, jumping (suspension bridge)

Platform G

- Sliding (steel slide)
- Sliding (metal pole)
- Hanging, moving (rings)
- Climbing (rope net)

Platform H

- Standing, sitting, viewing, climbing (mountain of spools)
- Stopping, pause from movement activities
- Stopping to make choices for next activities
- Standing, talking, dreaming
- Standing, deciding on new games
- Viewing the playscape and other children's activities
- Talking, sharing observations, planning

The following lists indicate examples of the number and type of linkages leading from each platform.

Platform A

- Slanted rope ladder to conveyor belt bridge
- Conveyor belt bridge to ladder and platform A
- Pulley off platform A to ground
- Ladder from ground to platform A
- Suspension bridge to lower level of platform B

Platform B

- Suspension bridge from lower level of platform B to A
- Ladder between ground and upper level of platform B
- Ladder between lower and upper level of platform B
- Tunnel from lower level of platform B to platform C
- Walk on top of tunnel from upper level of platform B to C
- Rope suspended from a steel pipe or upper level of platform B, leading to ground
- A half-circle sitting space under the deck, entered between posts

Platform C

- Tunnel to lower level of platform B
- Walk on top of tunnel to upper level of platform B
- Slide from deck to ground
- Step up/down to logs to ground or platform D
- Horizontal ladder to platform D

Platform D

- Horizontal ladder to platform C
- Step up/down logs to ground or platform C
- Two balancing beams to platform E: (one 3 by 6 inches and one 6 by 6 inches)
- Three options: step on both beams, step on wide beam, step on narrow beam
- Tire bridge to platform F

Platform E

- Two balancing beams to platform F
- Ladder between ground and platform E
- Rope net to platform F
- A triangular enclosed sitting space under its deck, with cutout shapes for entering, exiting, and viewing

Platform F

- Rope net to platform E
- Tire steps to/from ground
- Tire bridge to platform D
- Suspension bridge to platform G

Platform G

- Suspension bridge to platform F
- Slide from deck to ground
- Slide pole to ground
- Rope net to ground
- Hanging rings to platform H
- A rectangular, enclosed sitting space under the deck, with cutout shapes for entering, exiting, and viewing

Platform H

- Hanging rings to platform G
- Climb up/down mountain of spools

Construction

Construction of the Fountain Elementary School playscape took three months and was done during the summer school vacation. The earth movement, movement of trees, and landscaping were done by local contractors. Every attempt was made to take advantage of the natural features of the site, although there were relatively few as the site was for the most part a traditional hard-surface playground. One very large tree, however, was saved by moving it from the proposed site for a future building that would become part of the Central Park Community Center. It became the base for the children's treehouse on the playscape.

It was discovered that commercially manufactured play equipment could not be used in the playscape. No equipment was available that would meet all the requirements of safety and stimulation of the children's development that are necessary for an outdoor learning environment. Nor would any apparatus found in a catalog embody the specific plans and designs made by the children of Fountain Elementary School.

Thus, the designer created very detailed working drawings of the equipment, which was built by ten high school students working with two industrial arts teachers.

Post-occupancy Evaluation

Construction work was completed on the Fountain School playscape in September 1980. Although many existing trees were used, several years would be necessary for the playscape's new plantings to achieve full growth.

Nevertheless, the children of Grand Rapids began to use the playscape immediately and enthusiastically. For example, in the first year, attendance at a summer recreation program that had also used the original school playground increased form 3475 to 5576 people, or by 60 percent. Also, scouts, church/school groups, and other similar children's organizations now include a visit to Fountain School playscape on the their lists of scheduled activities each year. Playscape use has continued to increase, "attracting children and their families from other parts of the city and the metropolitan area, until it has become among the best known and most talked about children's playgrounds in West Michigan," according to Milton J. Miller.

The children who participated in the original design process continue to be proud of their accomplishments. They identify specific elements or apparatuses on the playground as their design ideas, even though the final architectural design may differ from the illustration or model they made during a design session. The pride of ownership demonstrated by these children is also seen in the absence of vandalism at the playscape. The children protect the playscape as their own property. For instance, at one time, the large mound in the nature zone was used for riding bicycles by the neighboring children, but students and parents became so concerned about the wear and tear on the turf that they voluntarily prohibited bicycle riding on the playground. Likewise, children planted hundreds of plants indigenous to Michigan in the nature center and kept the area around these plantings clear of all footprints.

Significant changes in the children's attitudes and behavior have also been exhibited on the new playscape. Many students who were frequently late for school before construction began to arrive early because they wanted an opportunity to play on the equipment before school commenced. Not only is the playscape inviting; it has promoted new attitudes. Fighting and quarreling over who was to have the next turn on equipment was a daily occurrence on the old playground, according to the principal of the school, Jim Sypniewski. On the playscape, Sypniewski notes, there is almost no conflict—"[it] encourages cooperation and sharing beyond my expectations."

Equally important is the safety of the new equipment. Contrary to what many observers said when the playscape was planned, it has proven to be much safer than catalog-purchased equipment. In the first two years of use, no bones were broken, and only one minor cut required suturing.

School administrators, member of the Board of Education, and parents have all expressed satisfaction with the playscape. Its cost was less than the cost of playgrounds equipped with manufactured devices, and there seems to be no limit to how the equipment stimulates the children's imaginations.

As the related community park and community center were completed in the following years, the Fountain Elementary School playscape has continued to provide a separate but nearby space for children to play in while older children, parents, and community members pursued their own recreational and educational interests.

Conclusion

The success of the Grand Rapids projects described in chapters 5 and 6, as well as others of similar character, demonstrates the value of providing beautiful, well-designed outdoor spaces that support both children's and adults' activities. Furthermore, it proves the value of involving both children and adults in the planning and design process.

Lately, there has been an increased awareness of the need for outdoor recreation spaces in towns and cities across the country, although these are primarily for adults. But not enough has been done. There should be more open spaces, particularly for children. This need is apparent in the instant popularity and use of such spaces as Central Park and the Fountain Elementary School playscape in Grand Rapids.

Playscapes do not have to be limited to the outdoor school/community site on which children play for relatively long periods of time. Play spaces based upon the principles discussed in this book may vary significantly in size, location, number of users, and general purpose. As long as the play space is safe and protected—offering the children a chance to be free, to explore, to develop their imaginations, to test themselves, and to unfold energy—it may be large or small, indoors or outdoors, designed for the very young or for the school-age user, intended for long- or short-term use, or be supervised or unsupervised.

There is a particular need for designed play spaces for very young children, from toddlers to school age. As with older children, their playscapes should be based on a thorough knowledge of play and of the child's physical, social, emotional, and intellectual development. Such a playscape for the very young can be built as part of the unsupervised community/school site described in Grand Rapids or in such supervised settings as daycare centers, nursery schools and kindergartens, elementary schools, and other educational institutions.

With the increased recognition of the value of play came the need for another kind of play space—the designed indoor area. Today, a few play spaces are provided for parents who need to "park" their children when they have things to do; more are needed. Indoor playscapes would be of great help in shopping malls, hotels, airports, hospitals, and other buildings where adults often take children when they are pursuing their own needs. In such environments, the play equipment takes on even more importance because of space limitations and generally shorter periods of use.

No matter what is required of a play space in terms of site, location, frequency and length of use, or the age of the users, *all* play spaces should be designed according to the principles set forth in this book. They should be based on the physical, emotional, social and intellectual needs of children of different ages; involve the users in the planning and design process; and use a variety of safe and attractive materials to construct as many activity settings as the play space can reasonably accommodate.

Bibliography

"A Play Space, Any Space." *Architectural Forum* 129:78–83. November 1968.

Allen, Lady Marjorie. *Planning for Play*. London: Thames and Hudson, 1968.

American Civic Association. *Play and Playgrounds*. Boston: Department of Public Recreation Leaflet #11, 1928.

Andrews, Sean and Ciaran O'Connor. *Space for Play*. Dublin: Comhchaideas, 1980.

Ash, Joan and Norman Sheppard. "Children's Playgrounds: A Visual Commentary." *The Architect's Journal* 145 (June 1967): 1409-12.

Bengtsson, Arvid. *The Child's Right to Play*. Sheffield, England: International Playground Association, 1974.

Benians, John. *The Golden Years: A Study in Child Development Based on the Work of Dr. Rudolf Steiner*. London: Anthroposophical Publishing Co., 1949. Especially: Ch. 7, "The Development of Willing, Feeling, and Thinking and the Child's Needs in the Three Seven-Year Periods," and Ch. 8, "The Young Child at Home and at School."

Central Mortgage and Housing Corporation. "Adventure Playground Information Kit 2." Toronto, Canada: Central Mortgage and Housing Corporation, 1977.

Curtis, Henry. *The Play Movement and Its Significance*. New York: Macmillan Co., 1917.

Dattner, Richard. *Design for Play*. Cambridge, Massachusetts: MIT Press, 1969.

Dewey, John. *The Child and the Curriculum*. Chicago: University of Chicago Press, 1902.

Dewey, John. *Democracy and Education*. New York: Macmillan Co., 1916. Reprint. Free Press Paperback Edition, 1966.

Dewey, John. "Progressive Education and the Science of Education." *Progressive Education* 5 (July–September 1928).

Duthie, James. "Play/Non-Play Determinants." In *The Anthropological Study of Play Problems & Prospects*, edited by David F. Lancy and B. Allan. West Point: Leisure Press, 1966.

Eby, Frederick and Charles Arrowood. *The Development of Modern Education*. New York: Prentice-Hall, 1947.

Elkind, David. *Children and Adolescents: Interpretive Essays on Jean Piaget*. New York: Oxford University Press, 1974.

Evans, Ellis D. *Contemporary Influences in Early Childhood Education*. New York: Holt, Rinehart, and Winston, Inc., 1971.

Friedberg, M. Paul. *Handcrafted Playgrounds: Designs You Can Build Yourself*. Random House, Vintage Books, 1975.

Froebel, Friedrich. *The Education of Man.* Translated by W.N. Hailman. New York: D. Appleton, 1887.

Gruber, Frederick C. *Historical and Contemporary Philosophies of Education.* New York: Thomas Y. Crowell Co., 1973.

Harwood, Alfred Cecil. *The Faithful Thinker: Centenary Essays on the Work and Thought of Rudolf Steiner.* London: Hodder and Stoughton, 1961.

Hogan, Paul. *The Nuts & Bolts of Playground Construction.* West Point: Leisure Press, 1982.

Hogan, Paul. *Playgrounds for Free: The Utilization of Used and Surplus Materials in Playground Construction.* Cambridge, Massachusetts: MIT Press, 1974.

Isaacs, Susan. *Intellectual Growth in Young Children.* New York: Schocken Books, 1966.

Isaacs, Susan. *The Nursery Years.* New York: Schocken Books, 1968.

Jacobs, Jay. "New Concepts for Playgrounds." *Art in America* 55 (November 1967):39–53.

Ledermann, Alfred, and Alfred Trachsel. *Spielplatz und Gemeinschaftszentrum.* Stuttgart, Germany: Verlag Gud Hatje, 1959.

Leland, Arthur and Lorna Higbee Leland. *Playground Technique and Playcraft,* vol. 1. 2d ed. New York: Doubleday, Page and Co., 1913.

Leonard, Fred Eugene. *A Guide to the History of Physical Education.* Philadelphia: Lea & Sebiger, 1923.

McCue, George R. "Candy Stripes & Polka Dots: A Critique of Contemporary Playground Equipment." *Landscape Architecture* 54 (January 1964):140–41.

Meyer, Harold D. *The Rural Playground.* Chapel Hill: University of North Carolina Extension Bulletin, vol. 1. no. 6, 1921.

Mumford, Lewis. *The City in History: Its Origins, Its Transformations, and Its Prospects.* New York: Harcourt Brace & World Co., 1961.

Noren-Bjorn, Eva. *The Impossible Playground.* West Point: Leisure Press, 1982.

National Association for the Education of Young Children. *Montessori in Perspective.* Washington, D.C.: National Association for the Education of Young Children, 1966.

Oren, R.C., ed. *A Montessori Handbook.* New York: Capricorn Books, 1966.

Pestalozzi, Johann. *The Evening Hour of an Hermit.* In *History of Educational Thought,* edited by Robert Ulrich. New York: American Book, 1945.

Piaget, Jean, and Barbel Inhelder. *The Child's Conception of Space.* New York: W.W. Norton & Co., 1967.

"Playground Sculpture—For the Fun of It." *Architectural Forum* 01 (November 1954):151.

"Playgrounds. With or Without Leadership?" Report of the Fourth International Conference of the International Playground Association. Paris, July 1969.

Plumb, J.H. "The Great Change in Children." *Horizon* 13, no. 1, (Winter 1971).

Rainwater, Clarence E. *The Play Movement in the United States: A Study of Community*. Chicago: University of Chicago Press, 1922.

Rice, Emmett A.; John L. Hutchinson; and Mabel Lee. *A Brief History of Physical Education*. 4th ed. New York: Ronald Press, 1958.

Rudolph, Nancy. *Workyards: Playgrounds Planned for Adventure*. New York: Columbia University, Teachers College Press, 1974.

Rusk, Robert R. *The Philosophical Bases of Education*. Boston: Houghton Mifflin, 1956.

Siegumfeldt, Max. *Byggelegepladser i Danmark*. Dansk Legeplads Selskab, 1981.

Steiner, Rudolf. *The Education of the Child in the Light of Anthroposophy*. London: Rudolf Steiner Publishing Co.,1927.

Steiner, Rudolf. *Lectures to Teachers, Christmas, 1921*. London: Anthroposophical Publishing Co., 1923. Especially: "The Knowledge of Man as the Basis of the Art of Teaching" and "The Child Before the Seventh Year."

Tolstoy, Leo F. *Tolstoy on Education*. Translated by Leo Wiener. Chicago: University of Chicago Press, 1967.

U.S. Consumer Product Safety Commission. *General Guidelines for New and Existing Playgrounds*. Vol. 1 of *A Handbook for Public Playgrounds*. Washington, D.C.: U.S. Government Printing Office, 1981.

———*Technical Guidelines for Equipment and Surfacing*. Vol. 2 of *A Handbook for Public Playgrounds*. Washington, D.C.: U.S. Government Printing Office, 1981.

Vance, Bill. *A Guide to the Development of the Adventure Playground*. New York: William C. Vance, 1971.

Van Dolen, Deobold B.; Elmer D. Mitchell; and Bruce L. Bennett. *A World History of Physical Education: Cultural, Philosophical, Comparative*. New York: Prentice-Hall, Inc., 1953.

Ward, Colin. *The Child in the City*. New York: Pantheon Press, 1978.

Index